"... if these buildings move me, they too must have life.

Thus the whole city is alive; buildings, people all are alive;

and the more they move me the more I feel them to be alive."

— John Marin

People & Places

Connections between the
Inner and Outer Landscape

JOHN R. MYER
MARGARET H. MYER

SP

Sandwich Publications
2006

東海道
五拾三次
之内
嶋田

Travelers fording the Oi River, Tokaido Road, Japan, c. 1832

This book is dedicated to our children.

Karimabad, a mountain village in Pakistan

This project was supported by a grant from the Graham Foundation for Advanced Studies in the Fine Arts.
Development for the initial idea for the book was supported in the 1980s by a grant from the Ernest A. Grunsfeld Memorial Foundation.

Page 1: John Marin (1870–1953), describing his response to the New York City landscape for Alfred Stieglitz's 1913 exhibit of Marin's watercolors.
Pages 2–3: "Shimada" from *Fifty-Three Stations of the Tokaido*, c. 1832, by Hiroshige (1797–1858)

Produced by Peter E. Randall Publisher for Sandwich Publications

Library of Congress Control Number:
2006901650

ISBN 1-931807-45-0
First Edition

Printed and bound in Hong Kong
Book design and typography by Bruce Kennett

The text for this book has been composed in Syntax-Antiqua, a printing type designed by the Swiss typographer Hans Eduard Meier. It was Meier's goal to make a modern type that could be read easily and without fatigue. To accomplish this, he based the letterforms of Syntax on those of the Renaissance types of Garamond and Aldus, but clothed them in the streamlined and minimal contours of a sans serif type. In addition, he gave the vertical strokes a very mild slant (3 degrees) toward the right, in the direction of the reader's eye movements. Syntax is one of a handful of sans serif types that can be used effectively for composing long texts.

Contents

Not only is the place of this dance a charming outdoor terrace on a summer's day, but also, in their dance each dancer forms a charming place for the other.

Introduction and Approach

Some time ago I asked my architectural students to describe a place or an event important in their lives and to share their reactions with faculty and other students. When my fellow instructors and I were taught architecture some twenty years earlier, we first had to learn to draw and to share through drawings. Only the master architect could say what touched him or what mattered. I wanted my students to have a different experience, using media with which they were already familiar, such as photography. I then wanted them to show to us, using words and images, how they saw and what they felt about the particular place they chose. After hearing some of the presentations, I asked my coauthor, Mart, a psychiatric social worker, to join me in an evening of student presentations at the school where I was teaching (Massachusetts Institute of Technology). The evening took the form of slide shows, each consisting of a series of images of a particular place. After the first one, the emotion in the room was so intense that nobody was able to comment immediately. We asked the presenting student to run his work again. This time, finding the group somewhat at a loss for what to say, I asked of no one in particular, "Why is it so difficult to talk about?" Mart said, "Well, it's difficult to talk about because it's like primary process thinking." We asked, "What is that?" and "What is secondary process thinking?"

We learned that the only thought process we are born with is the primary one, founded on inner needs. In time, we become aware of something besides ourselves: our mother's eyes or nipple or hand. This awareness of something other than us is the beginning of the secondary thought process. Over time we learn to cope with the world in this secondary way. The secondary thought process is conscious and rational, and is expressed in words and numbers. It deals with the world outside us and our relation to it. The primary process is unconscious or subconscious. It is expressed through allusion or analogy, and continues throughout our lives. The students' presentations expressed in pictures, slides, and drawings were analogs about how they felt about their chosen places. This was close to primary process thinking. Their presentations were not logical reasoned dialogues, which would have been closer to secondary process thinking.[1]

This explanation from outside our architectural world immediately caught us and found us thinking about these thought processes and their relationship to form and design. This work is an undertaking both to clarify and to share our still emerging views on the subject, through words and images. One thought above others has become important to us: We have the potential, in this period of canon-less architecture, to ground architectural form in perennial human need. In sharing the discussions we have had to form the perspective of our two fields — psychology and architecture — we seek to shed some light on how people associate with the physical world of places. We hope to interest audiences from our own fields, as well as others who influence the generation and uses of places, such as planners, developers, and politicians. Perhaps most important, we hope to reach those nonprofessional citizens who will make the places of their generation and who will influence the quality of places that are to come in the future.

Faced with the extensive system of associative thought that is ordinarily at work in both our waking and dreaming states, we have sought an approach that is significant to both the individual's life processes, on the one hand, and the places of his or her environment, on the other. In searching for a workable way to proceed with the exchange between us, we arrived at the idea that if we had a double-sided model, on the first from Mart's side — "what makes up a person" — and on the second from Jack's — "what makes up a place" — we could then have a dialogue about the possible connections that lie between them and about what, deep down, connects people and places.

The field of architecture has tended not to share its basic frames of reference with the general public or even openly with its own members. Rather, with a few exceptions, it seems that each practitioner holds the knowledge of the field in a proprietary way. The knowledge of architecture is transferred from practitioner to practitioner in their various forms of education, but rarely, if ever, to anyone outside the field, with an inherited, implicit understanding that each generation should continue in this way. Because of this condition, we have few models from which to choose to represent the basic substantive thought of either of the two fields.

In trying to find something to guide us and shape our dialogue, for the psychological side we decided on Erik Erikson's work *Childhood and Society,* in which he describes the "eight ages of man."[2] There are many studies of human development, such as Gail Sheehy's *Passages,*[3] but we could find no other work that combines psychology, anthropology, and sociology to describe a person. Mart chose to use Erikson's eight ages of man as a framework for her comments because it provides us with a geography in which we can locate regions of our inner landscape and explore their relation to the outer landscapes, and, more specifically, our built or planned world. As Erikson describes them in sequence, these ages of man are those of trust (achieved through attachment, continuity, and containment), autonomy, initiative, industry, identity, intimacy, generativity, and ego integration. (For a complete discussion of these ages, see appendix A.)

On the architectural side, I went through a series of my own thought pieces as well as a literature search to identify the form/design elements of place. There are two pieces of literature that I particularly valued: Kent Bloomer and Charles Moore's *Body, Memory, and Architecture*[4] and Kevin Lynch and Gary Hack's *Site Planning,*[5] as well as, to a lesser degree, several other works by Lynch. Although I draw from all of these, none seems to lay out the field in the way that we need. I have therefore drawn from my own experience as an architect and instructor of architecture to create a framework of the attributes of place.

As we proceeded with the approach we had settled upon and continued our exchange and discussed it with readers, the question arose as to whether the early ages of our lives really had a significant impact on later experiences of place. In considering this question, it seemed to us that the progression through Erikson's ages is really cumulative rather than discretely sequential, leading from infancy, to autonomy, to sociability when we join a larger society of the family and early school. Following the ages of initiative and industry, we struggle through adolescence to become young adults, and the cumulative sequence continues until the last age. Each individual experiences a particular age and passes from it and into the next in his or her own way. The culmination of these sequential experiences and transitions leaves the emerging person with his or her own individual imprint. Changes or differences that are apparently slight or subtle can affect the process in surprisingly significant ways. For example, aspects of the early struggle with our parents for autonomy may affect how we enter society, possibly carrying over into the later ages and into young adulthood and becoming — even in our balanced

maturity — a kind of personal signature as we enter the age of generativity. The perceptions of self that result from our cumulative experience of each of Erikson's ages would seem to be an important part of our experience of our world. Therefore, our experience of place is not separable from our present self or from the earlier ages that led to the present self.

Further, it seems that our perceptions of place have always been a part of us, in the sense that the hand and the mind are connected. We are always in that pairing of our individual selves and the place in which we find ourselves. We may variably like and dislike that place, or like one place more than another, and, if we are fortunate, have the opportunity to choose one more to our liking. But we do not have the choice of not having any place at all. We are never without a place. Thus, as we grow from one age to another, we are in an ongoing exchange with the place we inhabit. Here we learn to crawl, walk, sit, sleep, do an increasing number of things, and gain an ever-increasing understanding of what a place may be for us, and for our self within it. We come to understand that a place has a competence for human use, and we have a competence in the use of places. Place, then, from early to late stages of our development is another part of our being, a kind of twin. Deep in us lies the totality of our experiencing places, including those of our early experiences (even if they are only dimly recalled). We remember how it was to be awkward as a child. We are embarrassed when we fall down. We recall taking great pride in learning to ride a bicycle, to run fast, to climb a jungle gym or a piece of rock at our swimming hole, where we also found smooth places in which to lie or learned to swim in that sun-filled rocky pool. These experiences and their associated places are in us from those early beginnings, and our recollections of them may be aroused by a new place that alludes to the things that made the original experiences a part of us in the original place. When they are aroused, we have a visceral sense of having been there before, a sense that somehow seems valuable and marks that original place for us.

The early exchanges between us on the connection between self and place led us to recognize that habitat making is grounded not only in our inner psychological needs but in historical precedence as well. In these exchanges we have come to understand that this precedence is an agricultural one, some 9,000 years old. As best as we can reconstruct it, our architectural frame of reference at the beginning of the project was as follows: Modernism in architecture had effected an exciting and new beginning for those of us in the United States at the end of World War II — the time when I was in architectural school. Modernism projected a world of openness, mobility, light, space, and energy — a newness and creativeness that seemed like a new day following the darkness of the Great Depression and the subsequent World War. But in the couple of decades following World War II, it became clear that this new day also presented difficulties that needed to be addressed. Modernism had difficulty being responsive to the variable demands of clients, communities, regions, and cultures. It was a frame of reference that had an emerging commitment to an international style rather than a local one. Further, it was a frame of reference so unstructured and so without canons that it required a master to develop a successful form within it. Therefore, when modernism was applied to the practice of design of spaces, this did not result in a pleasing, ordinary habitat; habitats are not ordinarily designed by masters. Nor did modernism's involvement with the design of a single building readily produce a positive collective form of a street, neighborhood, village, or city. Rather, it offered a collection of separate objects, a bit like the human subjects described in David Reisman's *The Lonely Crowd,* a sociological study of American society.[6]

This frame of reference then led us to a longer view of our history of habitat making — that which came about in company with agriculture. What changed our habitats was the invention of agriculture as a more efficient source of procuring food than hunting and gathering. No longer did we have solely to hunt and gather as other beings did; instead, we could herd animals and grow crops as well. This enabled us to remain in one relatively fixed location, as opposed to the fluidity of location imposed by hunting and gathering. By being in one place, our fields of seeded earth became our fixed habitat, with built shelter for ourselves, for our animals, and for our stored food crops. The great part of our lives in the ensuing 9,000 years has been spent out on the land in our farms. While much of the architecture that we study, have come to love, and make reference to in the following text is not just that of farms, it does seem important to pay attention to the great preponderance of man-years spent in the agrarian habitat. One might guess that it amounts to 95 percent of all those man-years.

One striking aspect of farm buildings across the globe — and a reason for our attention to them — is the degree to which they share an architectural condition: a sense of harmony in their proportions and in their continuity with the land. This condition is apparently independent of culture, climate, topography, building materials, and the general form and size of buildings. The existence of such a commonality is not just our own view, but one

that a number of other architects hold as well. (We explore this later in the text, so will not elaborate on it here.) Given that the great preponderance of our habitat-building history was in the agrarian period, and given such architecture's use of harmony in its proportions and its continuity with the land, this seems a significant, stable precedent and one worthy of attention. We believe that this is the source of the relation of building to earth to which we have become accustomed and find in much of our traditional nonagrarian architecture. It continues as recently as in the work of Louis Sullivan, H. H. Richardson, Bernard Maybeck, Frank Lloyd Wright, and the brothers Charles and Henry Greene, as well as others. We also believe that this is the source of the use of harmonious proportions found in much of our architecture. Both of these ideas will be explored in this book.

The foregoing thoughts suggest that we are still a culture in transition from family agriculture to something else. As we find ourselves in the midst of this change, it is no surprise that we are having so much trouble generating our habitat in a life-enhancing and substantially meaningful way. Only in the last 150 to 200 years was family farming displaced by industry and "agribusiness," forcing our families to leave the farm. In comparison to the pace of the preceding 9,000 years, the rate of change in that brief 150 years has been disturbingly rapid. Perhaps we do not yet know — we have not yet figured out — how to express what it is that we need from our places in our constantly changing world. It is our hope that by exploring the connection between people and places in this evolving society, we will find a way to generate our habitat in a new and meaningful way.

A note about the illustrations
This book is also a place, with more than one dimension, and with views in many directions. Throughout the book, we will make reference to illustrations that may not be on the page you are reading; some you will have seen before and some will lie many pages ahead. All the visual resources for this book have been chosen with deliberate care, and we believe your understanding of the text will be illuminated to the greatest degree if you have time to refer to every example cited.

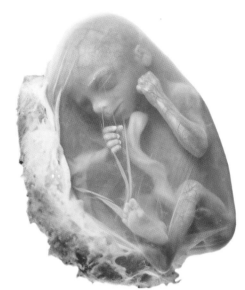

1 Our first place

Chapter 1
Connections between People and Places

Before we explore the connections between people and places, we must outline Erikson's eight ages of man. For our purposes, we have modified the ages (see appendix A).

Trust

    Autonomy

        Initiative

            Industry

                Identity

                    Intimacy

                        Generativity

                            Ego Integrity

2 *Frank Lloyd Wright's barn, Taliesin East, Spring Green, Wisconsin*

Trust: Attachment, Continuity, and Containment

The connection between people and places is the connection between our inner landscape and the outer landscape that we inhabit. When our outer landscape or "place" expresses our inner emotions, we respond positively. We start with our earliest infant need from the first "age" of man: *trust*. Trust is achieved by attachment, continuity, and containment.

In our early exchanges, as we considered our two frames of reference, we found ourselves turning to a question that had long been in our thoughts: "Why have farmers the world over built their farmhouses and other buildings so continuously with the land, and why does that continuity between building and earth still pervade impor-

tant portions of our work?" This turned out to be an important question, one that we touch on in a number of ways in what follows.

As we considered examples of places that have this continuity with the land, we thought of Frank Lloyd Wright's red barn at Taliesin East in Spring Green, Wisconsin (figure 2). We had seen this building together and had both been struck by the loveliness of the sight of it resting at the foot of a gentle hillside as it met a broad field of the valley bottom. The building evoked strong feelings within us. It reminded us of our earliest need, the need to be attached to "mother." The barn sits in the lap of the land, the lap of mother earth (figures 2 and 4).

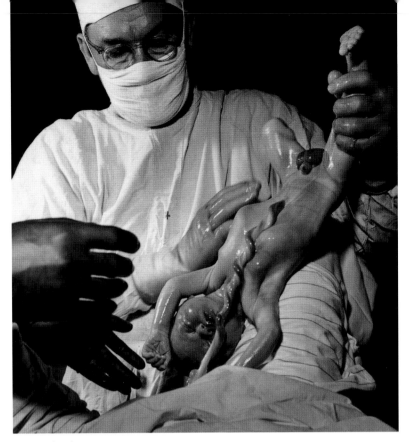

3 *Our birth*

Basic trust is the foundation for human growth and well-being. An infant develops trust by experiencing attachment to its mother (figure 5). Attachment in turn is achieved when the infant is contained and has continuous, consistent care. Attachment begins for us as unborn infants within mother (figure 1). Contained in soft comfort, at body temperature, with the reassuring rhythm of mother's heartbeat and the regular movements of her daily living, we are automatically fed through the umbilical cord, which connects us to her, attaches us to her. When we leave mother at birth (figure 3), we

5 *The beginnings of attachment*

4 *The beginnings of attachment*

arrive at the second place of our life. We are instinctively moved to regain that prior state: the containment, the warmth, and the rhythms of mother's heart and body movement. If things go well, we are successful in regaining this state in a new place in a mother's or father's arms (figure 4). We cling to mother, make eye contact with her, exchange sounds with her, and discover that we need to be fed (figure 5), and in general establish the beginnings of reciprocal relations with her. If we are fortunate, we become reattached.

As we grow, we have attachments to surrogate mothers: father, nurse, and other relatives. In this state of mind, over time we establish attachments to things (animals, artifacts, and places) as well as people: a favorite blanket or toy bear (figure 6); our crib or room; the house; its yard; the near neighborhood. We humans have so many attachments to others — people and things — that we are amazed when we see ourselves with all these attachments. Attachments tie us to a greater or lesser degree to our parents, siblings, colleagues, lovers, spouses, children, animals, and the artifacts and places of our environment. A world without such connections would be very different and unacceptably empty. An example of such a world is a ward for the chronically mentally ill, where individuals wander in their personal territories with no connections to people, things, or places.

Our world expands from infancy through the sequence of ages, as does the set of people with whom we form attachments. We may attach to members of the extended family: siblings, grandparents, cousins, uncles, aunts (figure 7). We are also likely to make attachments to our peers whom we come to know in nursery school, day care, play groups, kindergarten, and school. In time we form attachments to adults who become, in one degree or another, our lifelong friends (figure 8) or partners. By extension, it seems clear to us that in our environment, natural or built, we evolve attachments to artifacts, materials, and places. Like mother and those significant others throughout our lives to whom we develop attachments, these artifacts, materials, and places will also be there for us in particular rewarding and continuous ways.

In attachments between people and artifacts or places, there is an apparent exchange that may seem as rich as the attachment between people. For example, a visit to a childhood home may evoke an intensity that makes it seem like visiting an old friend. But in fact the attachment is one-sided: We are attached to these artifacts and places, but they are not attached to us. Hence the attachment is the consequence of our imagination: an association with a place. We associate with the place as a member of the family.

6 Early attachment to another: Christopher Robin and Pooh Bear

7 Another early attachment

13

8 Attachments in later life

9 *View suggestive of the sense of continuity between the New England farmhouse and the land*

As we explored this idea, it became clear that in our enthusiasm for attachments, we find ourselves perceiving attachments between things, as if the process of attachment formation was not only within us but also outside us. Not only do we find ourselves attaching now with one element and now another, but we also see these elements as having attachments and exchanges among themselves, as if they were a family or society with its own give and take, exchange, reciprocity. And again, in our imagination we associate to the connecting order that organizes these elements. There is a community of these elements, either one of our making or one that we inherited, in which there is a welcome companionship or aliveness.

When we looked at the harmonious continuity between the New England farmhouse and its land, we felt it was like the infant at the mother's breast. Both are an example of an associative connection between two physical elements that is given a special intensity; in each couplet, the smaller element is dependent for its being on the larger element: the infant on the mother (see again figure 5), the farmhouse on the land (figure 9). In the case of the farmhouse, the result is the architectural condition of continuity between land and building. (For a discussion on why farmers needed to build in such a way, see chapter 3.)

It is difficult to talk about attachment without talking about continuity, as continuity is essential to the forming of attachment. An infant becomes attached to a person when it has continuous care over time from that same person. An attachment to another evolves through an emerging sense of trust that this person will be there for us in a particularly rewarding and continuous way. When a mutual attachment occurs, both sides contribute to it. We see this in the ongoing dialogue between mother and infant, or between two people who are intimately attached. Such attachment comes about for the infant through a continuous relationship with the mother or other caregiver. Without continuity of care, attachment and trust do not develop. When there is no continuity of care, and therefore no attachment, the infant withdraws. Instead of trusting, he mistrusts. The infant guards against the loss of the caring figure and suffers intensely when it happens. The very small child, as he moves away from mother, drags with him some beloved object, an old blanket or a teddy bear tucked under the arm (figure 6). This object replaces the mother, giving him a sense of continuity with her even when separated from her. Homesickness often overtakes a child when he is separated from his caregivers. The break in the continuity of the relationship with his caregivers is the cause of this suffering.

This need for continuity in relationships with other humans also applies to our relationships to place. In the same way that we thrive in relation to our continuous caretakers, we become secure when our habitat is continuous and dependable. For a young child, moving can be traumatic (as it is for the elderly, who often die shortly after they are moved from their long-standing home). This yearning for continuity stays with us all our lives. We suggest that this is the source of our pleasure in visiting ancient towns and cities that still prosper, such as the New England village main street or village green with its surrounding farmhouses, barns, and sheds still at the

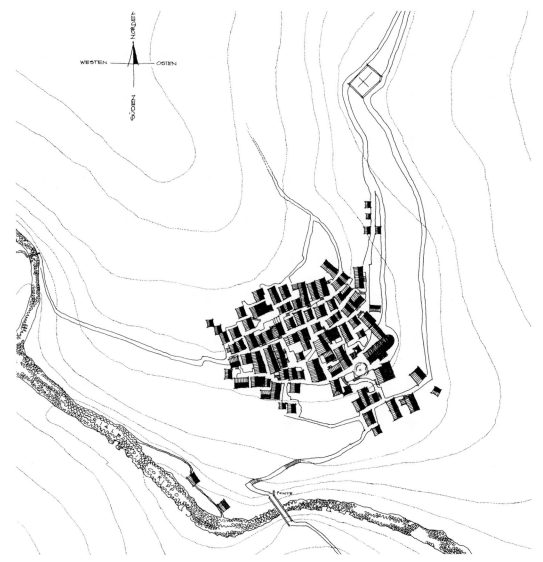

10 Site plan of Corippo, Switzerland, showing continuity of village buildings as if they were a flock

center of town. We take pleasure in visiting them not only because we find them beautiful, but also because we sense the continuous living, working, and caring that have gone on there for a century or two or three. It is one of the reasons that we are drawn to Italian medieval villages. (Another is the intimacy and containment of their narrow, winding, handmade ways.) They have continuously provided shelter and protection for centuries.

Examples of such communal continuities among a group of build-ings — mostly dwellings, in this case — are found in Corippo, a fourteenth-century village in southern Switzerland. Corippo lies at an elevation of 560 meters among mountains of 2,500 meters, just north of Lago Maggiore (figures 10 through 14). Corippo's popula-tion has fluctuated from a high of 550 in 1591 to a low of 42 in 1970. The communal continuities among the buildings of Corippo are several. First, these farmhouses have the same continuity with the land that all farmhouses have, and in this way have a shared continuity. Second, they are intimately close-packed, suggesting a sociable sense among them (figure 14). Third, they share a direc-tionality with the gabled ends facing north and south, "away from the weather." This closeness and shared directionality creates a lat-eral group continuity, keeping the buildings together in a way rem-iniscent of a flock of animals (figure 10). And fourth, they share a manner of building with thick masonry walls of split granite, wood-framed roofs of chestnut timbers, and planks covered with granite shingles. The lumber comes from a nearby valley.

11 View of Corippo from across the valley

12 Sectional drawing through Corippo village

Fortunately, this village has been marvelously recorded by four architects from Stuttgart. Their 1959 book describes the qualities of the village:

The houses are all of a similar type. They have two or three stories and an attic. The main living space of the house is usually located on the ground floor, where cooking and eating also take place. Bedrooms are located in the overhead stories. The attic serves as storage for wood and hay. Ventilation is often provided by an open gable facing the valley. Access to the upper stories is provided by outside steps. The small dimensions of the rooms preclude interior staircases. Rooms are rarely wider than 3.5 m, and ceilings are almost always under 2.5 m. . . . Interior walls are all stuccoed and whitewashed. . . . Large open fireplaces serve simultaneously for cooking and heat. Meals are eaten sitting on low benches in front of the fire. The lower one sits, the better the air quality. The draft of the chimney appears insufficient to draw off the smoke. Rooms are often smoky at eye level. A narrow opening is often left over the entrance for ventilation. . . . The agricultural inhabitants of the village have always led a harsh life. A raw alpine climate, the steep slopes of fields and pastures, and lack of soil fertility limit possibilities for development. Fields yield the minimum necessary to sustain self-sufficiency. Raising cows and sheep offered the only possibility for a modest supplemental income.[7]

14 Intimate winding ways of Corippo

13 The village fountain

The end result of these several continuities is one of togetherness of these structures. It is as if this village, sitting on the dauntingly steep mountainside, was a family with shared genes and frames of reference. The extension of the terrace retaining walls of the mountainside stone into the very building walls gives the powerful sense of the buildings being direct extensions of the earth, part of it, one with it (figures 11 and 13). In it we recognize our own need for such substantial, grounded, and communal spirit in our own habitat.

The infant's relationship to mother, the give-and-take of nursing, of eye contact, of verbal exchange, is what we call *reciprocity*. This reciprocity is part of the experience of continuity and attachment in the child's life (figure 15). It is the beginning of socializing and the give-and-take that we experience in our adult lives. Reciprocity is also an attribute of place. It is present in the New England farmhouse in its reciprocal ties with the earth, which parallel those ties the infant has to the mother's breast. The Katsura Palace in Kyoto, Japan, serves as another example (figure 16), in its relation to the adjacent pond and in the relation of both elements to the larger garden in which they sit. The flat earth of that portion of the garden is not left flat; rather, the void of the pond is in a reciprocal relationship with the part of the palace next to it, which the pond roughly matches in mass and size. This reciprocity links the palace not only to the ground and pond, but also to the extensive grounds of the garden and the highly expressive sense of nature that occurs there.

It is useful here to discuss continuity of place as an architect thinks of it. The continuity of place draws together several aspects of a place. First, there is the purpose of the place; second, the place's needs inform every aspect of the place with its purpose, providing a visual/physical/spatial cohesion in such a way that the parts of the design collaborate to achieve this continuity. Continuity might be thought of as establishing a kind of tonality of the place. If the continuity that is established is part of a larger or regional continuity, then the design may want to establish links with that contextual continuity and thereby extend its domain and presence.

Structures besides building can be involved in schemes of continuity: a garden, a street, a public square. The continuity we are describing might be, for example, what Monet so wonderfully depicted in his vast canvases of water lilies. With his brush he constructs an image where water surface, lily pads, blossoms, light, shade, and texture come together into one strong sense of place. This melding of the parts into one creates a sense of continuity. Such continuity may be embodied in the reciprocal relationship of parts, as in the Katsura Palace and its garden pond, or it might be a continuity that pervades

15 Reciprocity: a discussion between mother and child

16 Continuity in the reciprocal relation between the mass of the Katsura Palace and the void of the pond, Kyoto, Japan

a mix of landscape and dwelling, as in Wright's Falling Water (figures 17 and 18), which, like Monet's painting of water lilies, is a thing of great beauty and imagination. Architectural continuity, then, is about how one thing is recognizably a part of another and works with it.

17 Frank Lloyd Wright's Falling Water, view upstream (left)
18 Falling Water in its sunlit forest surroundings; here is a continuity (below)

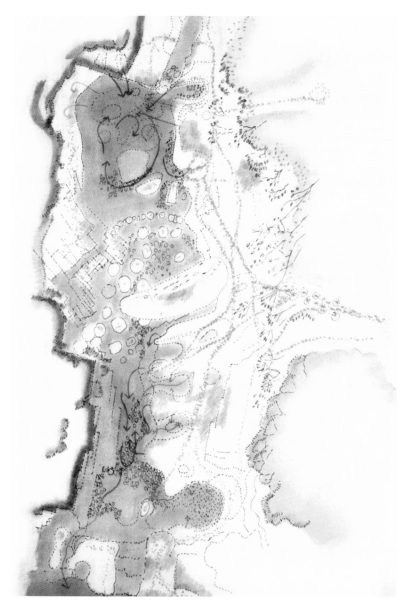

19 Sketch map of a swimming hole, showing water in blue

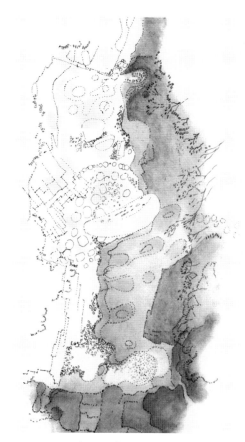

20 Partial map showing smooth surface at the edge of the swimming hole

21 Ledge under water

It also happens by chance that we find natural places whose inherent continuities touch us in a way that is akin to how our own man-made ones do. An example near where we live comes to mind. It is a length of the Cold River, a mountain stream on a remote portion of the southern slope of the White Mountains of New Hampshire, that has long served as a regional, communal swimming hole, called the Pothole. It is a place that has seemed to be one of my essential homes: a place to go when I want to feel particularly grounded. At one point I found myself needing to draw and write about it. Its several parts — smooth, warm ledges; rounded boulders and gravel; clear, cold, green-hued water; sun; containing trees and the containing sound of the moving water — cohere and form a continuity, a oneness of considerable force. I include a few drawings and photographs to share a sense of it (figures 19–26).

22 Ledge and small pothole

23 Boulders and gravel

24 Surface of large boulder at the middle of the swimming hole

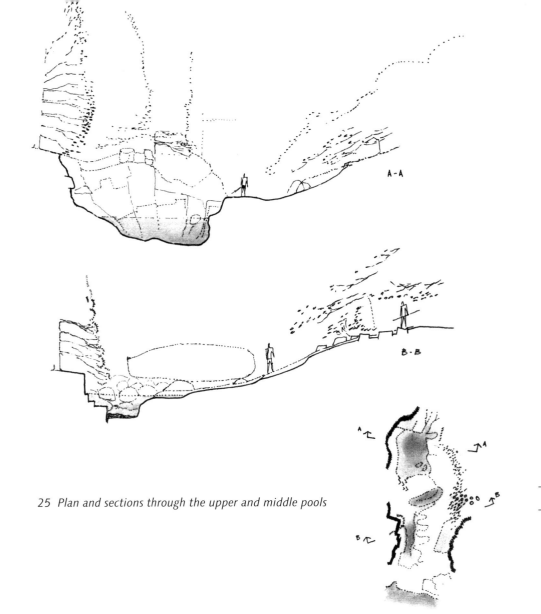

25 Plan and sections through the upper and middle pools

A-A

B-B

26 Water, floating leaves, boulder, and gravel

To this traditional understanding of architectural continuity we would like to add this thought: In a sense, the continuity of care that we experience in our childhood setting, with its nurturing and supportive contributions to our well-being, is giving to us, feeding us. This continuity of care is similar to the architectural continuity we experience in later life, which, when substantial, is giving to us, supportive, even nurturing in a subtle way. Here we are in the hands of another caretaker, the maker of the place, and delight in the offerings, at being fed.

There are a number of ways in which architectural continuity can be visually established. We will touch on a few here. There are those that occur because of closeness, such as adjacency, touching, clustering, coupling, and attaching and fastening. There are those that occur through sameness or opposition, such as sameness of material, color, texture, size, proportion, and shape or opposing colors and textures. Elements can share a spatial field or territory and thereby establish continuity. Then there is also the important attribute of reciprocity: the give-and-take, exchange, or dialogue between two or more elements. There are the formal devices for establishing continuity — for instance, deploying elements in such a way that they may be construed as a sequence, or as a theme and variations. Ordinarily, a number of these strategies are used at the same time in any given architectural setting, their appropriateness depending on the place maker's purposes.

There is another connection between place and our early needs, that of *containment* (see again figures 4 and 5). An important concern for us after birth is to regain the sense of security we had within

27 *Aerial view of the Piazza San Marco, Venice*

28 *The Piazza San Marco*

29 *Aerial view of Boston's Government Center complex and plaza, showing its vast uncontained space*

mother. Containment is vital to us, along with warmth, heartbeat, and rocking or another regular motion. As we grow older, we find ourselves needing less containment, but it will always be an important part of our need for shelter. The ancient reference "the hut in the storm" speaks of sufficient containment to defend against the worst adversity and keep us safe. At the least we may seek a defended place to sleep. At certain points in our lives, we may seek greater mobility and openness, and a shelter with less containment. But even with greater openness of shelter, we may still seek some degree of containment, from the trees or topography, hills or mountains, or our surrounding landscape. The essential associative sense of containment by a place of shelter is that of being held. This is a sense that we have known from our earliest beginnings. We have only to watch young children play to observe the seeking of this sense of containment. Children seek out cozy corners or overhanging bushes. They take their toy tanks under the bushes in front of the porch and battle one another in that contained space. On rainy days, they love to make houses out of card tables and blankets and play house inside their structures. As

grown-ups we may need less containment, but it remains a basic need throughout our lives (figure 58).

Containment also offers one particular reason why we so delight at being in the Piazza San Marco in Venice (figures 27 and 28), whereas Boston's Government Center Plaza (figure 31) leaves us cold. We feel contained in the former and exposed in the latter. We approach the Piazza San Marco through Venice via winding narrow pathways that lead past shops, over bridges, along canals, and across small squares until we explode through a colonnade into the great space of the square itself, entering through the square's narrow fourth side. Across from us at the far end is the glistening San Marco Basilica, flanked by the ducal palace, with the Campanile, the great brick tower, to the right and the clock tower to the left. On either side of the long flanks of the square are colonnades with shops and cafés. Pigeons fly about. People stroll, shop, feed the birds, and sit at cafés where they talk or listen to music (figure 28). The buildings are handsome and although there is architectural variety in the ducal palace, the Basilica, the Campanile, and the clock tower, each differing from the other and all at one end of the plaza, the other three sides have similar architecture.

Boston's Government Center Plaza is also a space of great size, with Boston City Hall, a powerful, handsome building, sitting in it. In contrast to the Piazza San Marco, however, the space of Government Center Plaza is variably and incoherently defined on its four sides, with each of its corners open to streets leading away, thus bringing about a sense of not being contained by the cityscape (figures 29–31). Only when we compare one of our urban public spaces like Boston's Government Center Plaza with a place like the Piazza San Marco do we discover how uncontained our American urban space truly is, and to what degree it leaves us exposed and uneasy.

23

30 *Proposed changes to Government Center, with the intent of making the space more comfortable and contained*

31 *Pedestrians in Government Center Plaza*

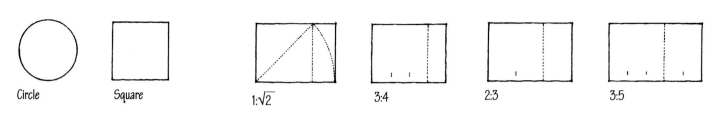

Circle   Square   1:√2   3:4   2:3   3:5   1:2

Before we depart from the issues of attachment, continuity, and containment we should address *harmony, conflict,* and *proportion. Proportion* is part of a broader thought process that goes on in our daily lives regarding our food, our clothes, our activities, and our habitat. It is the process through which we balance the various things that make up our lives — more of this, less of that — in a number of interlocking ways. A great majority of these ways have to do with the ongoing action of our living and that of those close to us, relatively independent of place. Still, an important number of them have to do with the use and arrangement of our habitat.

Much of our habitat making lies in our agrarian past. As we pointed out in the introduction, only in the last 150 to 200 years of the roughly 9,000 years of agriculture and the habitat building associated with it have humans engaged in other than predominantly agricultural activities. During most of that agrarian time, the farming population sought to mitigate its exposure to agricultural disaster by seeking support and avoiding anger from the gods. One of the approaches they used was to show their harmonious intent to those gods in all ways, including the harmonious forming of their habitat. Thus, the condition of harmony has been central to our habitat making throughout history. And it seems that harmony is achieved largely by means of proportionate thought, through which we adjust things to become what we sense to be proportionally correct. We will now enlarge upon the issue of proportion and harmony, bearing in mind that there are uses of proportion other than for the achievement of harmony alone. A kind of superficial harmony may be achieved by making everything the same. However, a harmony of significance both to us and to our forming of places, as in the case of the farmer, is one that is achieved in the presence of conflicting tendencies. As we discussed earlier, this is a harmony achieved in the interest of supporting ongoing life, such as the farmer's very survival, and thus avoiding the cost of unresolved conflict. It is the harmony sought between a child and his mother.

At about the age of two, the child begins to assert his independence. He exercises his own powers, deciding what to do and when he will do it. In asserting his independence in this way, he comes into conflict with his mother. Achieving harmony requires real invention by

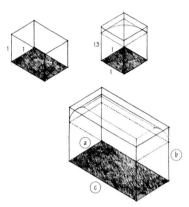

32 Palladio's plan shapes and heights of seven ideal spaces

both parties, but mainly by the mother. She needs to give the child room to explore and test his newfound independence. Later, he will develop his own adult identity and begin to seek intimacy and partners in life. He may marry and have children and again experience conflict. With luck, he will undertake to resolve these conflicts harmoniously.

Such harmony is much valued in our lives, and this value is the source of our seeking the presence of harmony in our habitat, both built and natural. That which is proportional and harmonious touches place making in a number of ways. We seek to have what we feel to be the right balance among the complement of elements that make up a place. We work at the multiple issues of more of this/less of that to achieve a number of thematic purposes, such as cost, firmness, sustainability, and architectural expression. We also find ourselves working to achieve the appropriate proportionality of the spatial order of a place, its sub places, and the elements that make it up. And as we do that, we are also working at establishing the proportionality of the relative sizes of their component parts and those sizes relative to our own dimensions, or what is referred to by architects as *scale*.

We do not know where the sense of proportion that we inherit and consider harmonious comes from, but it clearly goes back in some part to the ancient Egyptians and Greeks. However, proportions

33 Parthenon, Acropolis, Athens

34 Parthenon, Acropolis, Athens

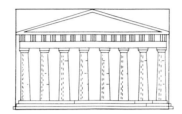

35 Elevation of the Parthenon with
the golden rectangle overdrawn

36 Diagram of the Parthenon façade by
Peter Smith

affect how we feel about a room, a window, a doorway, cabinet-work, or a piece of furniture. Proportions are an important part of how we feel about a place. Palladio (1508–1580) proposed several ideal plan shapes for rooms that he describes as the "most beautiful and proportionable manner of rooms" (figure 32), taken from his *Four Books on Architecture* (1570).[8] He also proposed several methods of determining the proper heights of rooms, so that a room's height would be in proper proportion to its length and width.

In understanding the grounding of harmony, we need to examine examples of the compound forms that make up our built places, in which harmony is achieved in the resolution of a conflict. Such conflict is exemplified in the tension between the longer and shorter dimensions of the rectangle, and its resolution is thought to take place in the square and the golden rectangles (figure 32). The tension between the length of the sides in the rectangle is resolved by the sides' being of equal length in the square. In the golden rectangle, the same tension is resolved in a different way, in that the two different lengths form a rectangle that many have found beautiful. The golden rectangle is shown overlaid on the elevation of a Greek temple (figure 35).

A third example is found in Peter Smith's discussion, in *Architecture and the Principles of Harmony,* of a conflict or contest between two forces in the façade of the Parthenon. The columns of the façade (figures 33–36), according to Smith, "represent repetitive vertical forces counterbalanced by the strong horizontality of the base or crepidoma, the entablature above and the pediment, in which the horizontal component is much stronger than the vertical" (figure 36). He goes on to describe the façade as "a contest between two opposite but related classes of information taking place within a system which reads as a single major unit. Wherever there is a jux-taposition or clash of two information networks, the mind seeks to establish an orderly relationship. When it succeeds there is a basis for harmony, but where it fails there is a dissonance." He continues, "In this axial contest in the Parthenon the horizontal principle is victorious, due to the combined weight of pediment, entablature, and crepidoma. Dominant prevails over subordinate."[9] We have in this analysis a harmoniously resolved contest, one that is akin to those harmoniously resolved conflicts in our life processes that we have discussed above. By presenting Smith's analysis, we suggest that the harmoniously resolved conflicts are alive in us and are also a general condition in the form of our built habitat.

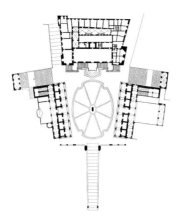

37 *Plan of the Capitoline Hill, with its Piazza Campodoglio, Rome*

38 *Approach ramp to the Capitol and the Piazza del Campodoglio*

39 *Section through the Piazza del Campodoglio*

We need now to address another aspect of proportion: our sense of relative size in a place. We gain such a sense by the relative sizes of the elements of a particular place. This is often referred to by architects as *comparative scale*. The Piazza del Campodoglio, on the Capitoline Hill in Rome (figure 37), served as the civic center of the city in Renaissance times. We enter the piazza, a space of size and importance, by means of a long ramp (figure 38). We immediately have a sense of some intimacy despite the size of the two flanking buildings with a dominant, somewhat elevated, central building at the end of the piazza (figure 39). This intimacy, which was probably an appropriate feeling for the leaders of Rome to experience in this seat of power in the sixteenth century, is achieved through the use of a giant order — giant in the sense that the columns that make up the two flanking buildings are two stories high rather than the traditional one story. The columns and the buildings they support, designed by Michelangelo, represent the first use of a giant order, with the purpose of making the visitor feel large in a large space, and thus empowered. The columns and the roof that caps the buildings (and, in a sense, joins the columns) are the central elements of the architecture. There is nothing else of any size with which to identify, and the columns, like us, are vertical. Thus, just as Michelangelo intended, the visitor immediately identifies with these columns that are large with respect to the place, and he feels large himself. To feel large in a large place is to feel powerful and, in Bernard Berenson's words, this is "life enhancing."[10]

Although the achievement of harmony may be one of the most important uses of proportion, we should note that there are other valuable uses to which proportion may be put. A brief exploration of Libeskind's Jewish Museum in Berlin may be to the point (figures 41–43). This museum is visually striking and terribly painful to see or think about. The form of the building is primarily that of a

40 *View of the Piazza del Campodoglio*

41 *Overview of Libeskind's Jewish Museum, Berlin*

radically zigzagging way or corridor that one thinks might be galleries in time but are for the most part empty. The primary exhibit is the building itself, in a way not dissimilar to that of other expressionistic museums.

The pattern of the building's linear corridors or long, gallery-like spaces is an urgent zigging and zagging, much like the path of a cornered animal just before the kill. The spaces seem to have no other immediate architectural purpose in their zigzag order. And we find that the corpus of the building mass, enclosed by an industrial-like metal skin, has slashlike openings, glazed, but seeming like wounds from some giant external sword. In some places the wounds aggre-

43 Interior gallery, Jewish Museum

42 Exterior elevation, Jewish Museum. Note the juxtaposition of an established form and the forces that would destroy it.

gate into greater areas where we can see the inner tissue of the corpus. Other than the hacking and piercing from the outside, there seems to be little of an inside–outside exchange. That which is inner is inner and that which is outer is outer. In both, there is an absence of a sense of life.

The formal architectural order of the building has only a few key attributes in our terms: mass-space, path-linearity, shape, and proportion. (By *mass-space* we mean the composition of placed masses and the spaces that are formed between and around them.

Path linearity refers to the pathways we arrange through and between building masses.) The proportions of the building of mass-space are elongated and organized around corridor-like spaces. There is only one broad place in this elongated structure of narrow corridors where one is asked to stay, and that is the central lobby. The principal outside court space is notable for its sense of absence of life or an artifact that would support life. It is barren where we see a breadth of exterior wall; we are asked to focus on the damaging slashes in a barren place. It is an architectural territory of terror, attempted escape, wounds, death, and absence of life. We have put forward the Jewish Museum in Berlin to establish the thought that architectural expression in places can involve a broad range of issues. It can be, as in the Campodoglio, the setting for the governance of Rome in the sixteenth century, with all the pomp, circumstance, and energy at the center of the city. Or it can be a testimony to the Holocaust in Berlin in the twentieth century, with all its brutality, terror, grief, death, and barrenness.

Autonomy

In the previous section, we have associated early infancy needs — attachment, continuity, and containment (Erikson's age of trust) — with places and found that these early needs become a part of us and profoundly affect how we make places, perceive places, and react to places. This leads us into an exploration of Erikson's subsequent "age" of life, *autonomy*, and its bearing on people and places. If an infant has experienced sufficient attachment, continuity, and containment and thereby has gained a sufficient sense of trust, he can move on to the next stage in his development and begin to exercise his own autonomous will. In a typical infant, this comes about at an early age. An infant initially sees himself as part of a whole — in fact, as the center of the whole. As he grows, however, he realizes that he is separate from others. He learns that in addition to the "me," there is a "you." With this knowledge the child learns that he need not be totally dependent upon his parents, that he has options, and that he can begin to control himself and his environment. He has the power to make decisions: to dress or not to dress, to eat or not to eat, to defecate or not to defecate, to step in a puddle or not to step in a puddle (figure 45). This ability to feel that he can control and has choices about himself and his surrounding is vital to his development. Anyone who has been involved with a toddler (also known as the "terrible-twos" child) can attest to how intensely the child needs to assert control over his environment. As he finds ways to exert such control, he gains self-confidence and a sense of well-being. A child who fails to successfully engage and traverse this stage of development may find himself confronting lifelong feelings of discouragement and helplessness.

As a result of our struggle for autonomy, later in life this same independent, autonomous, confident spirit that we develop forms some part of our adult identity — at least we hope it does. It may also become a part of the places we create for ourselves and affect the way we relate to them. For example, if we look at Kasimir Male-

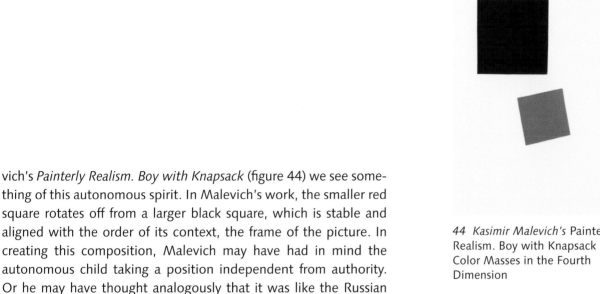

45 *The age of autonomy*

vich's *Painterly Realism. Boy with Knapsack* (figure 44) we see something of this autonomous spirit. In Malevich's work, the smaller red square rotates off from a larger black square, which is stable and aligned with the order of its context, the frame of the picture. In creating this composition, Malevich may have had in mind the autonomous child taking a position independent from authority. Or he may have thought analogously that it was like the Russian Communist Party splitting off from the staid traditional order of the Russian czarist governance. Similarly, we may recognize the same condition in Frank Gehry's renovation of his own house (figures 46 and 47). The kitchen skylight seems to have sufficient independent energy and independence of form from the remainder of the house, in which it seems as if it might at any moment — like a large transparent cube or die — take off and roll down the street. Our mind's immediate interest is in rooting perhaps for, perhaps against the part's autonomy, or simply in observing that there is tension between part and whole, between autonomy and belonging. Even in adulthood, long after our child self has resolved the issue, it is very much part of us.

In this separation of the part from the whole that the child confronts as he is working out his need for autonomy, there is no suggestion that the whole can or should be reconstituted or deconstructed as a result of the part's struggle toward autonomy. Such a reconstruction or deconstruction would be too great a task for our two-year-old even to imagine — or for anyone to imagine when confronted by an overwhelming authority. Rather, it represents the search for room on the part of the child so that he can begin to make decisions for himself. Despite his seeming brave autonomy, he is of course deeply enmeshed in the support of his parents, as is the Gehry kitchen skylight in its surrounding house. We delight in the child who asserts his autonomous self, although his parents may despair. In the same way, we delight in places that assert their autonomy without overpowering the environment.

44 *Kasimir Malevich's* Painterly Realism. Boy with Knapsack — Color Masses in the Fourth Dimension

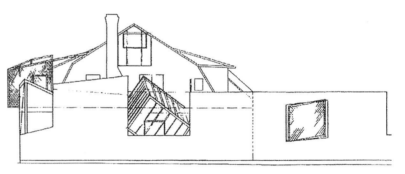

46 *Elevation of the architect Frank Gehry's house*

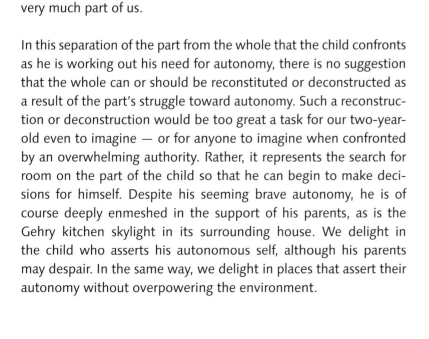

47 *Autonomous kitchen skylight, Gehry house*

29

48 A "permanent" modern encampment, a kind of autonomy of place

For a stretch years one such autonomous place existed in Moulton-boro, New Hampshire. Let's go back in time to visit it in person, so we can better understand its qualities.

On Bean Road there is a field of perhaps an acre at an elevation slightly above the road (figure 48). It is bounded by a stone wall — an ordinary feature in this part of the world, where farmers had to clear fields of stone so that they could be mowed and cultivated — now overgrown with vegetation and blending into the landscape. The field is open to the road but otherwise surrounded by a mixed woods of deciduous trees and pines. It has an outlook over the wall and main road to the east, with low, rounded mountains, largely forested, beyond.

On this pleasant mowed field sits a well-positioned, beautiful, shiny mobile home with a glass door facing east to the view. It has seemed, as we have considered the scene over several years, that the owner has established a kind of permanent encampment and it is this juxtaposition that is of interest to our discussion of autonomy. We say "encampment" because what has evolved in this field is a modern camp, a mobile home on rubber-tired wheels with a hookup to drag it away, and because it has a Johnny-on-the-Spot — one of those plastic, portable toilets rented and maintained by vendors — placed over against the back stone wall of the site on the west edge of the field. Furthermore, the outside sitting area, just in front of the glass door of the mobile home, is composed of those aluminum and canvas folding chairs that we typically take to picnics or the beach. A green canvas awning is extended on hot days from the mobile home to give shade to the chairs (and presumably to those sitting in them). The mobile home has a buried electric and telephone hookup all neatly connected to the utility pole at the edge of the dirt and gravel driveway. This driveway breaks through the stone wall and provides vehicular access to the field (though it stops well short of where the mobile home is parked). The occupants' car, when there, is neatly positioned on the grass in line with the mobile home. It is clear from all of this careful arrangement and attention to the needs of human occupancy that the owners of the property could pack up their camp on a moment's impulse. They could leave with their mobile home behind their car, calling on their cellular phone to the vendor to remove the Johnny-on-the-Spot as they roll down the driveway. It seems more permanent than temporary because it has been here now for several years, summer and winter, although it is used mostly in the summer. It also seems permanent because the locations of the various elements have been very carefully considered and are now rather fixed, with a real architectural sense of position, mass, and space. It seems perma-nent, too, because it is well cared for. The field is mowed, more like a lawn than a field. Every item on the property is well maintained.

The tension in this field between these two extremes — temporary camp and permanent habitat — is palpable. The setup has the autonomy of a boat on a sea of land. There are houses and even farmhouses that approach this quality as well. They do not dream on the earth as does Wright's barn (see again figure 2) or the New England farmhouse (see again figure 9), but they sit on top of the land, independent of that land to some degree, providing a clean, neat, well-stocked cabin within.

The realization of our human need to assert our autonomous selves led us to the discovery that not only does this need affect the places we make, but it affects the way we respond to places as well. This seems to be one of the reasons that some places succeed and others fail. The age of autonomy is not just about separation or defiance. It is also about independence and being in control. The two-year-old who begins to assert his independence is not so much defying his parents as he is seeking control, autonomy, and the right to make decisions for himself. This quest is vital, and with any

luck stays with us all our lives. When directed to do something by an overwhelming force — that is, when we perceive our right to make decisions for ourselves being trampled upon or taken away — we may respond in a variety of ways, depending on the circumstances, becoming conforming, passive, frightened, angry, hysterical, or assertively autonomous. The architecture of Nazi Germany (figure 49) played on this central theme — so alive in us — with its vastly powerful hierarchical order that bids us to conform absolutely, to give up our autonomy or leave secretly. Furthermore, as we consider certain high-rise, concrete-slab habitats, it seems to us that the main reason they failed to provide housing that anyone wanted to live in is that they do not allow their inhabitants to control their own environment. These slabs, which are found the world over, leave little room for a person to control his environment and to make it his own. They subordinate the person, disempower him, and deny his autonomous self (figure 56).

49 *Hierarchical architecture of Nazi Germany, disavowing autonomy*

50 *In school, learning to write*

Initiative and Industry

In the foregoing we have explored the second place of our existence and its great driving need to overcome the loss of the first place, within mother, and to become strongly reattached to her. Then, with sufficient attachment, containment, and continuous loving, we see the child's need to become independent and exercise some autonomy. If he achieves this autonomy, he enters the third age, *initiative,* and then the fourth age, *industry.* In these ages the child gives up his struggle for omnipotence and joins society; he becomes civilized. He now sees himself as part of a family, which in turn is part of a larger world. As he gives up his struggle for omnipotence, he seeks to gain his parents' love and approval by becoming like them and by becoming a useful member of the family. He takes the initiative and joins others; he dreams of becoming like his parents, whom he emulates. He attempts to gain recognition and satisfaction by producing things and gaining skills, knowledge, and competency. Hopefully he is now trusting and confident enough to learn to share and be sociable. He is ready to begin school, to learn, and thus to become industrious (figures 50–55). As the child grows and learns to be a part of a family and the world beyond, he learns about a range of houses, gardens, yards, fences and gates, paths, sidewalks, and streets that are a part of the world outside his immediate experience. There exist a whole range of materials about him, and he must get acquainted with each and discover its individual identity. He learns that the brick sidewalk in front of the house is not good for roller skating but is fine for riding a bike. The stone and gravel path to the side door is not good for either. Some gates are easy to open; others are sticky and squeak. The corner store has candy. He learns that some parts of this world

are private, some are public, and some are in between. In some he is welcome; in others he is not. He learns that some parts of this world are quite safe and some are dangerous, such as moving cars and trucks, big dogs, and gangs of bigger boys. He learns that some portions of this world feel good and some do not. Early on, portions of the neighborhood, the school, the park, and the shops that feel homelike reassure him. He is drawn to those good places where there is a range of opportunities to do things: run into other kids; play games; try new skills such as riding a bike, playing ball, and being sociable.

He learns through direct experience and education that there is a certain order to this world. There is a system of grouping or clustering, and there are paths connected to each other. For example, houses are grouped along streets. Classrooms are grouped around paths or corridors. Shops can be clustered around a bus stop. In addition to the groups and clusters, there is an overlaying or underlying system of extensive networks made up of streets for pedestrians and vehicles, and utilities such as telephone, cable TV, water, sewer, gas, and electricity. There is the earth, with its geography, topography, and geology; its flora and fauna; its climate and its seasons. There is the diurnal pattern of day and night. In many countries there is the system of public and private ownership of the land. There is the social order between ourselves and those with whom we coexist: family, teachers, friends, and acquaintances. There is the knowledge that this social order has developed, and may include reading, writing, and arithmetic, or it may include hunting, farming, herding, or minding younger children. There is the system of mores, economies, and laws of the community, which are there to maintain a civil order among us. To understand all of this is a major undertaking.

51 *Boys getting household water, Karimabad, Pakistan*

52 Reading

53 Reading to each other

As the child grows, he learns and understands more and more about his environment. With this understanding comes the ability to read it. It becomes more and more legible to him. The more legible the environment, the more the child can understand it, engage it, and make use of it. In addition, the more options the environment offers with respect to what he can do and is interested in doing, the more he can make use of it, and thus the more his competence will grow. At the same time, the environment will evoke a sense of competence in and of itself. According to urban designers Kevin Lynch and Gary Hack, "Places should have a clear perceptual identity: be recognizable, memorable, vivid, engaging of our attention. It should be possible for the observer to relate identifiable features, one to the other, making an understandable pattern of them in time and space."[11]

Here we would like to focus on the issue of the environment's being "vivid." For a child to grow and learn, an environment needs its coexisting elements to have intensity, in their individual presence as well as in their juxtaposition to each other as they make up the form of the place. That is, in one of a wide variety of ways, it must give the child a sense of texture, color, relative size, light and dark, heavy and light, changeability and immutability, organic and mineral, moving and fixed. Further, in the juxtapositions of this broad range of conditions there must emerge, in the form of the place, a sense of aliveness that interests the child, draws him to it, engages him, and in a way becomes alive to him as well as to us.

The opposite of this is in evidence when no care has been taken in the arrangement of the place, and because of this its complement

and juxtaposition of elements have few of the above conditions and meaning and therefore are dull to the child and to us. In such an environment there is no breadth of what might be experienced by the child eager to learn in all kinds of ways. It offers him only a limited world. If the place does not have an intensity or vividness at least as strong as that of the child's ordinary life intensity or aliveness, then it is a dull acquaintance, not a vivid companion, and not a good place for him or her to spend time. The places of our contemporary world contain much in which there is little of this intensity or vividness.

33

54 Harvesting

55 *Learning to hunt*

And finally, the geography of place that emerges over time in the child's mind — composed of topography, climate, weather, directionalities, territories and ways to travel, natural and built elements — needs not only to be legible to the child, but in addition should achieve an order that enables it to be intensely felt. For example, if a house is strongly homelike and sheltering, both within itself and in its surrounding yards, with shade trees, fences, lawns, and gardens, then the street that runs in front of it, with shade trees arching over the road, can extend that sense of shelter. The sense of a house sheltered is extended to some degree to the street, particularly if the opposite side has a similar order of shade trees and tree-surrounded houses. We think here of intensely felt childhood memories of summer shade, and of winds from winter storms moving through the branches as they shelter the houses from those winds.

To illustrate this early need for intensity, I will tell you about an early memory of my first remembered neighborhood, on Avon Hill in Cambridge, Massachusetts. It existed between our half of a dou-

ble house at one end and my nursery school on the other, a short walk along streets lined with trees and houses. I started going to nursery school when I was about three. My mother and I would walk for about a block, then we would cross the street, looking both ways, and turn a corner to the left. The next street was narrower and sloped up to the top of the hill only a few houses away. When we reached the top of the hill, again we turned to the left, and went up a steep and very narrow dirt way, like a country road, until we got to the top, where we found the gate to the school in a vertical board fence higher than my head. There were usually several mothers with children my age talking outside the fence. Through the gate, the yard appeared large and nice, often sunny, with a sand floor, and swings and jungle gyms, and lots of children doing all kinds of things. Some were kids I knew. Across and at the back of the yard was the shingled school with green trim, which seemed very like a house. You walked into a small corridor lined with cubbyholes, for coats and boots, one of which had my name on it. From this entry were two classrooms, each with large windows with small panes that let in a lot of sun. The classrooms were nice and somehow like rooms at home. That is the whole neighborhood I remember from that time: our home at one end, with the narrow, tree-lined streets and a couple of left turns to get to nursery school. I liked both ends and the walk between. The going from one to the other was an important and interesting trip.

For another child in another culture, such a trip is a path for getting a day's supply of water for the family (see again figure 51). In rural Karimabad, Pakistan, children venture along a curved path beside a narrow canal that bends horizontally around the middle of a natural bowl occupied almost wholly by narrow agricultural terraces. These terraces, stepping down the steep slope and curved to follow the shape of the bowl, are planted with wheat and other crops. After a bit, the path turns uphill and, in time leaving the terraces behind, travels up through steeply sloped grazing land to a spring high above the bowl. These children learn the way from older siblings at a very young age and proudly fulfill this vital task each day. The paths between home and spring are clear, beautiful, and safe. It is a delight for these young children to venture out, to perform an important task.

This environment in Karimabad enhances the child's need to take initiative and be industrious. With the help of my mother, eventually I was able to walk to school on my own and thus was also able to take initiative and be industrious in this sense. Both the walk for water and the walk to school are simple and clearly defined. They are on a scale that a small child can comprehend. Furthermore, they are safe, and each is filled with vistas that can engage a child. Within the very limited understanding that the child has of "what the larger world means," the child feels as if he is a functioning citizen in that world.

These places are far different from a home in which the child lives on the twelfth floor of a public housing slab on the edge of a big city. Leaving such a home to travel to school, the child must take the elevator down to the street and then walk, usually for some distance, before arriving at school. He walks through a landscape with few amenities, dominated by large, bare parking lots and occupied by groups of older children who may or may not be friendly. He is too small either to understand the huge "slab home" he leaves or to be able to safely cope with it or the environment around it (figure 56). He cannot manage the trip to school from this home and through this environment on his own, and it is a major chore for his caretaker to guide him through it each day. His environment thus limits his ability to initiate, explore, and become industrious.

At an older age, a child is able to recognize richer and more complex patterns of buildings, streets, and pathways. In contrast to the smaller elements like streets and buildings that may define a place for us in heavily developed areas, in more open places such as farmlands, our place may be partially but importantly defined by large elements such as mountains, hills, valleys, rivers, and lakes. The definitions provided by these elements help us to feel oriented. We have all experienced pleasure in places where we know where we are and how to get from point A to point B without feeling lost or being harmed. Such places give us confidence not only that we can manage getting to our destination, but also that we can initiate the journey and make our way on our own. These are places whose size does not overwhelm us. They may be very large and dense places, but they have parts that we can relate to, such as trees, plants, benches, small walkways, front steps, and courtyards. These are places where we sense a reason for a particular order, and we are familiar with this order and sense that it is meant for us. We are drawn to cities, parts of cities, and places that empower rather than subordinate us.

In summary, what we have discussed in regard to the ages of initiative and industry is the child's work to achieve enough competence to permit him to cope and manage in his world, and in the places that make it up. Reciprocally, the places that he needs (as do adults) are places that are "competent" in the ways we have discussed, so that the inhabitant may exercise his powers in them.

56 *Slab housing*

Identity

The fifth age, that of *identity,* is the integration of all of the previous ages. The task of the adolescent and young adult is to achieve a sense of self, derived from a positive integration of the past, that is essential to his ability to create and produce in the future. During this stage of her development, the young adult separates from her family and becomes her own woman. At the same time, she incorporates the values of her family and her society into her own value system. By the time she is an adult, she should have gained an identity, "a sense of self," and should be able to see herself as a separate and unique person, with internalized values, memories, desires, and dreams.

Human identity is an evolving process through which we attain an appropriate degree of inner control, self-awareness, and a sense of where we have come from and where we are going. A person with identity has an inner core, an inner sameness or consistency that results in his having a sense that he is who he is no matter where he is or with whom. Individual identity also assumes that our internal self is the same as what the outside world perceives. Erikson noted, "The sense of ego identity, then, is the accrued confidence that the inner sameness and continuity prepared in the past are matched by the sameness and continuity of one's meaning for others, as evidenced in the tangible promise of a 'career.'"[12] A person who has successfully developed a sense of identity knows where he comes from and has come to terms with his past. Perhaps most important, he is "legible" to others and "distinctive." When we meet him, we sense who he is and where he comes from: We can "read" him. He is autonomous, innovative, and purposeful. There is a consistency between his inner self and his outer expression of self. It is worth noting that long before our young person emerges as an adult with an identity, he has taken on the physical erectness of carriage that will eventually mark him as a member of the adult community he is joining. He now adds to that erectness a recognizable way of meeting the members of that community, through accepted patterns of relating: making eye contact, shaking hands, and exchanging ideas. One has only to compare the adolescent who slouches about, avoids eye contact, and lacks social graces to the young adult who relates with directness and confidence to realize the long leap from childhood to the adult person with an identity (see figure 57).

We have summarized the qualities of the young adult with identity. Certain things stand out: autonomy, self-awareness, correspondence between inner and outer selves, distinctness, legibility, purposefulness, confidence, and "erectness." We now need to ask, What are the attributes of place that relate to human identity? When we talk about place, we are talking not only about natural places, but also about places that are man-made and have grown haphazardly, as well as about places that have been "designed." Examples of natural places that have an identity are the Italian Dolomites and the Lakes Region of New Hampshire. The steel mills of Youngstown, Ohio, and the textile mills of Manchester, New Hampshire, are places with an identity. The Piazza San Marco and the Guggenheim Museum at Bilbao, Spain, designed by Gehry, have an identity (figures 28 and 148).

What do we mean by *identity of place*? It derives from a place's form, which in turn derives from the attributes that make up that form. Ordinarily a place will have many attributes, all of which contribute in some degree to its identity: spaces and masses of things such as buildings and plant materials; enclosures and openness; bigness and smallness relative to people; horizontality and verticality; light and dark; color; texture (smoothness and roughness); materials (wood, mineral, metal, glass); organic and/or inorganic things. It is often the case, however, that a few of its attributes will have special emphasis in the forming of its identity.

One such attribute is *spatial order*. Space is necessary for us even to be able to occupy a place. If a place lacks sufficient space for us, we cannot be in it. Space is the domain of our life's activity, including the arts of dance and sculpture. *Mass* (another attribute), along with the ground, is that which defines space. It is the surface of mass and ground that defines the extent of space and gives it shape. With its materiality, mass is most like our bodies, but unlike our bodies, it may last a long time, measured in eons as opposed to years. Spatial order derives from the interconnection and reciprocity of mass and space; it is located in space and time.

The hands and minds of those shaping a particular place form that place's identity. Like a person, a place or environment has identity because we imbue it with essential human qualities such as "attachability," "likability," and "harmoniousness." We do this with artifacts throughout our lives. And further like a person, a place's identity is complex, and when it has a distinct character, it draws our interest more so than when it does not. The reverse is also true. A place of uncertain form disturbs us, just as a person with a disoriented character, or a person without identity, may disturb us.

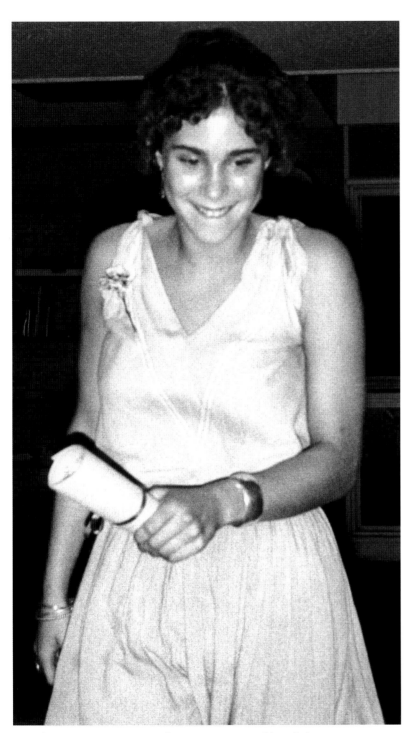

57 Identity: a young woman having just received her diploma

A place that has its own identity is reassuring to us. In such a place, we feel oriented. As in the case of human identity, the place needs to be clear about what it is, what it is derived from, what it expects to become, and how it is to be perceived by those about it. It must be coherent; if it is to be successful, this quality of identity needs to pervade its extent. It needs to be distinctive, legible, and expressive of its identity. This quality of identity should also be capable of being epitomized in such a way that the whole can be rendered in a simple sketch or other image, or in a few words, as that famous architectural prototype is rendered by the phrase "the hut in the storm."[13]

The hut referred to in "the hut in the storm" is a shelter that even without the storm gives us every assurance that we will be well defended there, can survive the worst there (see figure 58). Its identity must have to do with the taking care of those who seek shelter there through its expressed and actual capacity to defend those within its walls against bad weather. It is an identity that seems to have been expressed best in the past in a robustness of roof, walls, and foundation, as in the log cabins or stone mountain huts of earlier days in the United States. Other examples are the Appalachian Mountain Club shelters and the shepherd huts in high pastures of Greece and Norway. The identity of these structures is easily recognized in the singleness of the structures' purpose and their elemental, life-preserving nature. We respond immediately and affectionately when we come across such a hut. Shelter is also a very significant theme in architecture. Shelter — the thing that contains and protects us — is ordinarily found in ancient forms of building.

Let's review the characteristics of the elemental hut, in the context of our criteria for the identity of place developed above. If a hut is successfully designed, then we will easily read it for what it is: a robust, small shelter, one of a long line of shelters in which we can feel fully protected in the event of bad weather. Its form tells us that it is of the region in which it is located, and anyone of that region would be able to read it at first sight as being of its culture. It is clear what it is, what it is derived from, and how it will be perceived. (And perhaps its future is also clear.) Its smallness, simplicity of purpose, and construction epitomize the same kind of coherence that exists in a more complex manner in larger buildings. Here we have epitomized a safe space, robustly defended. The same stones or logs are seen both without and within. It has the coherence of an inner and outer sameness. Its distinctiveness and legibility derive from both site and region. The site and the building traditions of the area will determine, for example, whether stones or logs will be used in its construction. They will also determine the pitch of the roof, the way its doors and windows are arranged, and the material used for the

58 A hut with identity

floor. Its identity is clear. Similarly, in the hands of a competent builder or designer, its sheltering qualities may be rendered with intensity.

Although it may seem all too simple to design such a building, it is in fact easy for incompetent hands to get it wrong. Rather, it is because of its simple and profound nature that it is useful to us as an example in the matter of identity and place. It is worth mentioning that in earlier times, buildings such as a hut for the shepherd and a house or barn for the farmer were erected in the tradition of the previous generations. They learned from their forebears and used local materials, and the structures were "raised" by the builder and his neighbors. It was a time of architecture without architects. The "hut in the storm" appeals to us because it has, when it is well "designed," a clear identity. Anything that has "identity" is appealing to us, but the hut also appeals to us because its quality of shelter and protection speaks to our early needs and dreams. We are safe in this sheltering hut.

Houses hold the same appeal; for many of us, a house is the place where we began and where we become. A house is typically larger and more plural and complex than the hut. Like the person who occupies it, a house accumulates memories. The accumulation of memories, of people, places, events, becomes part of our internal world and gradually gives us an identity. Like us, a house has memories that become ritualized, that express feelings and give it an identity. In discussing the making of places, Bloomer and Moore comment, "To diminish the importance of the body's internal values is to diminish our opportunity to make responses that remind us of own personal identity, responses we may have had as children when we were playing house or exploring the outdoors."[14] Thus, in order for a place to enchant us, it must have identity; this identity of place reaffirms our own internalized values, our own sense of selves, our own identities. A well-crafted house will express memories that are like the internal feelings of a person, a body. By doing so, the house becomes habitable.

A place that we love to come upon, a place that we head for, also has a sense of identity: for example, Harvard Square in Cambridge, Massachusetts, the North End in Boston, a country store in a rural village, and even some suburban malls. The Piazza San Marco, discussed earlier in this chapter, is a place with a powerful identity (see again figure 28). It is the central communal place of the city, the place where it displays armed might, its religious celebrations, and its daily life. As Kevin Lynch describes it: "Highly differentiated, rich and intricate, it stands in sharp contrast to the general character of the city and the narrow, twisting spaces of its immediate approaches."[15] Although highly complex, it is legible, distinctive, and visually rich. Its vast space is contained and defined in such a way that when we enter the square, we know that we have arrived: Here is the heart of the city. Lynch noted that San Marco is a setting that "orients its inhabitants to the past, to present rhythm, and to the future with its hopes and dangers."[16]

A place that has no identity frightens us. Here we feel confused or lost, just as the young adult feels afraid when he has no direction, no purpose, no connection to the past or hopes for the future — he has no identity. Where there is no harmony between us and the outside world, we feel disoriented. This can be understood easily when we look at dull or ugly places such as the endless "roadtowns" (figure 59). While these endless roadways or strips may provide a service of convenience for people living near the road with their multiple offerings of undifferentiated convenience stores, auto centers, motels, and fast-food restaurants, they leave us with little sense of place. They were not conceived as a place where we might want to spend time or come to love. Rather, the unconnected array of cheap structures that characterize "roadtown" have no center, no quality that we might meet, no identity! Instead, they are places where we come, not to linger but to conduct business and leave. Survival is the mode when in this realm. Like roadtowns, high-rise public-housing slabs are hard to live with and not "life enhancing." For those who inhabit these slabs, there may be no other option. Many are forced to raise their families and spend a lifetime in them. And like the roadtowns, these high-rise housing slabs were not conceived of as good places for families to be. It is not possible for a mother to go about her chores when her children are playing outside.

If the children are on their own outside, they are subject to the frightening activity of gangs. High-rise slabs are often desolate. We feel subordinated by their height and overwhelmed by their mass, small, insignificant, and powerless. Since there has been no investment in the arranging of the place so that it might be one that we could love or feel good in, there is no identity here (see again figure 56). These public-housing slabs with no human qualities of place are so dangerous to live in, and result in such dysfunctional families, that some of the buildings have been razed.

59 Roadtown, a place with little sense of identity

60 *A Japanese wedding*

61 *A pregnant woman*

Intimacy and Generativity

The sixth and seventh of Erikson's ages are those of *intimacy* and *generativity.* After a young adult gains a sense of identity, he seeks to fuse it with that of others. He is ready for intimacy, which Erikson describes as "the capacity to commit himself to concrete affiliations and partnerships and to develop the ethical strength to abide by such commitments . . ."[17] Through his or her capacity for intimacy, the young adult may take a "marriage" partner with whom he or she can mate and conceive babies (figures 60–62). Another expression of intimacy is in evidence when an individual takes on a "business" partner to form a law firm, a manufacturing industry, a service industry, or an architectural practice. These unions are often intimate and they can be productive, creative, and generative. Thus, one doesn't have to marry and have children to have intimacy and be generative. For many it is not just children that make them generative; it is their art, music, writing, law, teaching, dancing, gardening, buildings, cooking, and service to others (see figures 63–65). We seek intimacy not only with people but with places as well. Intimacy is the adult form of the attachment we sought from infancy. As children, we were drawn to intimate spaces and cozy corners. Adults also seek intimate spaces. The alleys in Corippo (see again figures 13 and 14) and the narrow streets of Boston (see figure 125) please us. In our habitats we make intimate nooks or seating about a fireplace.

62 *Several generations of an American farming family*

63 A partnership, Einstein and Oppenheimer

64 The Anna Myer Dance Company developing a new dance

65 A painter at work

Generativity, the putting of the next generation in place, both by having and raising children and by making cultural contributions, is a central purpose of our lives (see again figure 62). It is not surprising, therefore, that it should find its way, among our other interests, into our place making. It does so in several ways. Perhaps the most important is through the influence of the places of one generation on the places of the next. Our own places have enough richness in them, enough identity, character, and intensity, that the next generation understand the uses of place and can continue to make places as a valuable resource in their own lives, habitat, and ongoing generativity. Members of this next generation may revere the past by making it a part of themselves. That does not mean, however, that this generation must copy the past. It need not copy, because the past has become part of us. It is thus inherently expressed in the new or the present. It is like the child who separates from the parent or the adult who separates from the past. Both internalize and incorporate the "parent" or the "cultural values and styles." Now, living as their own selves, they are free to create new places for the present, which look to the future. As Josef Albers put it, "In art, tradition is to create, not to revive."[18]

Herbert Muschamp describes this process of separation from the past and internalization of historical values, form, and styles when he writes about the new Rose Center for Earth and Space of the American Museum of Natural History. "Whatever your feeling about the old planetarium," he writes, "you cannot accuse the new one of lacking long-term historical memory. The design is saturated with it. This is a mature modern building, a structure unafraid of revealing the deep roots from which modern architecture arose. The design's historical awareness far exceeds that of buildings that merely ape period styles."[19] (Figure 66.)

A place should not only express its historical past and look to the future; it also needs to be economically adapted to the next generation and even possibly to the one after that. This adaptation may include incremental change over a range of conditions, such as spatial organization, use, density of development, and other attributes of its form. Furthermore, a place should be technically adaptable to changing needs, and demonstrate an expectation that it may be changed in the future without a great loss to its identity. The easy flexibility of the medieval town fabric to incremental change comes to mind. It is a flexibility that is a property both of the individual structures and of the public ways and places that occur between them (see again figures 13 and 14).

Too, the DNA transfer to the next generation that occurs in human generativity might reasonably find its analog in the design of place from one generation of place makers to the next. There may be a recognizable imprint, or form or style, establishing a meaningful continuity. The underlying continuity of our agrarian past, discussed earlier, has carried with it a deep imprint in the form of the farmhouse through many generations. In New England villages, we still see the Cape-style farmhouses built in the seventeenth and eighteenth centuries. This style, with adaptations, is prevalent in new construction today.

66 *The Rose Center for Earth and Space at the American Museum of Natural History, New York City, by the Polshek Partnership, Architects*

67 *Barn suffering loss, New Hampshire*

Ego Integrity: Wisdom, Loss, and Restitution

With the passage of the seven previous ages of man, writes Erikson, "[o]nly in him who in some way has taken care of things and people and has adapted himself to the triumph and disappointment adherent to being, the originator of others or the generator of products and ideas — only in him may gradually ripen the fruit of these seven stages."[20] This last phase of life Erikson calls *ego integrity,* which he describes as an "emotional integration which permits participation by followship as well as acceptance of the responsibility of leadership."[21] The relationship between adult integrity and infantile trust is that "healthy children will not fear life if their elders have integrity enough not to fear death."[22] Ego integrity is the end of one life cycle and it actually concludes in the next generation, in our children or in the products or ideas of our creativity. As Rita Rainsford Rouner puts it, "In becoming parents we become participants in the ongoing humanity, links in the chain of generations joining an unremembered past to an unforeseeable future. Through our children and their children we know ourselves connected to dimensions of reality to which we have no direct access ourselves."[23] With the next generation in place, or with the products of our creativity in place, we can accept our mortality, as we are assured of our continuity.

In considering the above, generativity is one way that people deal with their own mortality. The life experience of *loss and restitution* is another significant factor in our lives and in the places we

68 *Funeral, a part of grieving*

69 *Loss is evident in burial grounds such as this one in North Sandwich, New Hampshire*

70 *One-hundred-year-old shingles on a building showing loss*

inhabit (figures 67–73). Loss and restitution are not directly included in Erikson's eight ages of man. How do people deal with loss, and how do places take loss into account? As we discussed above, in the broad array of people and things in our lives with which we become attached, there occurs a network of attachments that in a sense become the place of our lives. From this network we find ourselves losing links: now this one, now that one. It is an experience in which we suffer intensely. In the case of losing car keys, it may be only a moment's upset, remedied by putting our hands on a backup set. In the case of such a lifelong attachment as the loss of a close friend, parent, or child, it can be a matter of deep suffering for a substantial period. It is an experience all of us undergo increasingly from birth.

The human process for dealing with loss is grief. By grieving we go through deep inner processes that, when we have done them sufficiently, come to an end. At such a point we find ourselves substantially restored. We gain restitution, the act of being restored. The experience of grief is painful and changes our perception of ourselves and of the world around us. During the grieving process, the world seems to become less bright, less hopeful, less susceptible to our intervention — at times the world is bleak and dark. Within ourselves we feel disoriented, without purpose and energy, and with a kind of inner emptiness and pain. Grief, like an unwelcome guest, comes on its own, stays seemingly forever, and finally leaves — and blessedly, all of a sudden, we feel like doing something for the first time since the grief arrived, and find that it is, to some important degree, gone.

We will describe the grieving process in some detail as it has implications for how we are with others and how we relate to places.[24] Grieving is a process that takes time. When we have loss, our first reaction is to deny the loss. Next we try to "undo" the loss by saying, "If only I hadn't done this, then that wouldn't have happened." Then we become angry, next sad, and finally, if the process is not interrupted, we become accepting through our internalization of that which we have lost. Although denial is a normal first step in the grieving process, it is important that we not linger in this stage — that we do not try to cling to our denial. When small children experience loss or trauma, grown-ups often try to protect them from the accompanying grief by "helping them to forget." They say, in regard to the child who has lost a parent, "She's too young to go to the funeral" or "Don't talk about the deceased as it will just upset her — she needs to get on with her life." Actually, the very opposite is true for the child (and for an adult experiencing a similar loss). Children need to talk about the lost parent, see pictures of him, tell stories about him, cry about the loss, and be angry at the dead parent for dying. By doing these things, the child internalizes the lost parent, feels comforted by this, and gains a kind of peace.

There are many kinds of losses, such as the loss of youth, of beauty, of a job, of family (through divorce or death), of country (through war or disaster). Uncomfortable as it may be, loss is an important part of our lives. If we recognize the ways in which children and adults grieve, we will better understand that places, too, need to acknowledge loss. As people need reminders of the person, object,

71 Restitution can occur when a decaying building is repaired, as in this New England barn.

72 New England farmhouse and barn, both well repaired and the farmhouse brightly painted

or country they have lost, so places need evidence of what has gone before. Boston's Freedom Walk and the Holocaust memorials are attempts to provide just that. They are places that incorporate reminders of the past. An environment that is rich with places of the past and has workable places for the present is a valuable one; when we are in such an environment, we do not exist in just the present but also have deeply felt connections to the past.

Surroundings that show evidence of loss in themselves, such as weathering, wrinkling, discoloring, and structural settlement (see again figures 67, 69, 70), have a kinship with us. It is akin to our own bodily experience of loss, and thereby to other experiences of loss — for example, loss of a friend or loved one. As such, there is at least a place to be with the loss. The difficulty that we are having in dealing with our loss is not unique to us. Other people have experienced loss and endured to know better times. We find similar relief in the distress of natural and built things: the weathering of trees or rocks in the landscape, or that of the shingles and clapboards of a building. In surroundings that do not recognize loss, life is more difficult. In the absence of friends or acquaintances or in a built world that does not evidence loss, a whole world of our experience is not recognized in our surroundings. Even during a period in our lives in which grief is not at the forefront — in which we are not actively grieving — such a place will seem less significant, empty of one whole part of us.

But it is not only loss that is present in our arranged environment: An untended or decaying building makes us most uncomfortable.

The deserted barn with a hole in its roof can expect no renewal, only further decay and collapse (see again figure 67). What is absent here is not loss, for there is plenty of that, but rather remedy for loss. If we undertake caring repair of a distressed building to which we are attached, we have provided it with a remedy for the loss it has suffered. We gain restitution for the building; it is restored. The process through which the building is restored to soundness — and perhaps even beauty — is analogous to the grieving process we undergo in the loss of human attachment. Through the internalization of the person we have lost that takes place when we grieve, the person becomes part of us and we gain a kind of restitution for the loss. When we first see the New England farmhouse with evident distress, weathering, and settlement, and then see it carefully repaired and brightly painted, we feel comforted (figures 71 and 72). With its bent and gnarled form, the Japanese bonsai tree typically displays an epitome of the distress that comes with age. It also displays a sense of grace that is beautiful. Through this juxtaposition of distressed age with beautiful grace, it suggests a good way to be with age. Although this is not easy to achieve, whether in the form of the tree or in our lives, if we can gain such grace, there is a way to go, a possible restitution in the time of old age.

In addition, we suggest that the issue of loss, with or without restitution, exists, of course, not only in our agrarian past, but also very much in our urban/suburban present (see figure 73). It is in the buildings of our urban/suburban present, its ways, its places, and its artifacts. Substantial buildings of massive stone or other masonry, in contrast to wooden farmhouses, seem impervious to loss because of their thickness and durability, yet over time they show discoloration and erosion, the patterns of water coursing down their surfaces. They darken with city dirt, becoming at times almost black. They settle now and then, more or less and differentially, showing cracks in their masonry. They may at times hold water in their walls, causing rapid deterioration within and without. Despite their size and heft, we associate their loss with fear and their caring restoration and cleaning with relief. And in this process, we perceive the building to be durable over great lengths of time, because it will take so long at such rates of erosion for it to be done away with. Through this perception, the building gains a certain greatness in our eyes. It will last a very long time despite the losses it sustains, very much longer than we will.

In the urban/suburban world, it is not just buildings that speak of loss and restitution, but also the ways and places on which they front. In some parts of a city or suburb, the ways will be largely well

73 Urban loss without restitution

repaired. In others, there will be less care and repair, and in some, little or none (figure 73). The evidence of disrepair and neglect is familiar: the bent and rusted signpost, the broken street lamp, the cracked sidewalk and curb, the unevenly paved street, the unpatched excavation, the pothole, the dead tree. At the sight of these visible signs of decay — as with the farmhouse with the hole in the roof — we are uncomfortable.

In some areas, the level of neglect and decay is even more severe. The definition of the public way is rendered less clear with the disappearance of a building here and there. In some places this disappearance is more pronounced; perhaps it has advanced to the extent that there is the loss of the sense of containment given by the buildings on the street. Roger Trancik refers to this loss of order in the city as "lost space," space no longer defined.[25] *Lost* is a good word to describe such a non-place. In these places we have lost the sense of physical order by which the city is made, the public way. For most of us who need a working city — and ideally a comfortable one — to get on with our day or our lives, this loss is as deeply threatening as is untended loss. For a few courageous and entrepreneurial people, this abandonment may be an opportunity for new endeavors of city building. For others — street people come to mind — it may be a place of temporary encampment or of crime.

To perceive loss in a given architectural form, we need to sense a subtraction from the prototypical body of the form. In the examples mentioned above — erosion due to weathering, staining, cracking, and the adjustments from differential settlement — all are a part of the ordinary work of the building. They are also akin to the ordinary human losses that come with age: weathering, wrinkling, the frame settling differentially. A more life-threatening loss for a building is the subtraction of a portion of a roof or perhaps a hole in a wall.

With respect to the way such loss is remedied, because we need to identify with the processes of loss and restitution in our surroundings, it is important that we repair architectural form in such a way that we recognize both the loss and the repair in the consequent repair. For example, a masonry wall showing signs of failure might be repaired deliberately with a stone of somewhat different texture or color from the original, thus building evidence of the repair directly into the portion of the wall affected. This suggests that in the conceiving of the wall's form, the design took account of its eventual failure and repair, and was comfortable with it. Such a design enables the wall to carry the increasingly rich message of having expected much experience, and of having survived it gracefully, in the course of its life.

Chapter 2
Implications for Design of Places

As we expanded on the themes developed in chapter 1 and discussed them with readers and colleagues, we concluded that it would be useful to show how designers might employ such themes in their designs of places. We have chosen three places of our own design at three different scales that made use of these themes. First, at the house scale, is our own dwelling in North Sandwich, New Hampshire (1987–88); second, at the scale of a small village or campus, is the design of two dormitories in central Massachusetts (1972–73); and third, at the urban scale, is the initial urban design for the Boston Government Center and the downtown Boston waterfront (1959–64).

The urban projects occurred well before we began to develop the thoughts in chapter 1; the dormitory projects took place during the time we began our discussions that led to this book. Most of the themes of chapter 1 — trust (attachment, continuity, containment), autonomy, identity, and generativity — have long been a part of architectural thought. It should come as no surprise to find their presence in these prior urban projects. What is new is how the themes of chapter 1 are grounded in us and in the places we make.

The Pasture House

The Pasture House (figures 74 and 75) was built to accompany an existing, much loved, camplike house on an old family pasture going back a number of generations. It lies in North Sandwich, New Hampshire, on a south-facing hillside with approximately 15 percent slope. The pasture covers ten acres, roughly a thousand feet long across the slope and several hundred feet up and down the slope. Below this lies twenty acres of woodland and then beyond is the view of the ancient, glacier-rounded Ossipee Range, which is vast and powerful. This new house was designed for our use in retirement. The camp house was given to our children. Originally the pasture was kept clear of bushes and trees by cattle. Later, when the cattle disappeared, brush cutting kept the pasture open. The ten acres of open land that make up the pasture never became a

74 Site plan of Pasture House (new), new barn, and old house showing path connection and continuity

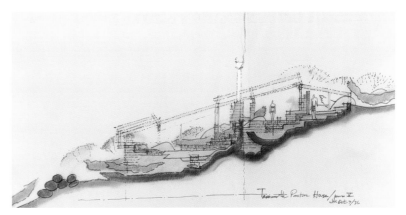

75 Section through Pasture House: an early scheme showing the uphill–downhill orientation of the structure

76 View from Pasture House, looking southeast

field. There were too many large boulders for oxen and stoneboats to move. Only today, with our giant backhoes, are we able to clear these stones to make a field that can be mowed.

The space program for the house was small: a living-dining-kitchen space at its center, a large screened porch for summer living adjacent to that center, an outside terrace, a garden adjacent to the porch, and a potting shed adjacent to the garden. Also near the center is an entry, a carport, storage for wood, and guest parking. Three other spaces were included: a bedroom; a study/guest bedroom/TV room; and a bunk loft for grandchildren to sleep in and have as their own place. And of course a bath, a toilet, a laundry, and considerable storage were also included. Our desks were to be worked into our bedroom and study, one in each. It was thought that the house should be as much a part of its site as possible, including its form, landscape, microclimate, views, and pathways out across the land and connecting us to the old house some four hundred feet away uphill and to the east. With this sense of connection to the site, we wanted to use passive solar heating and cooling to the greatest degree possible. The heating derives from the sunlight that falls on this patch of ground. The cooling results from the southwest summer winds and the temperature of the earth itself some feet below, carried upward by the masonry into the house.

We selected a site that protrudes a bit from the general sloping plane of the hillside, giving it a slight prominence over the surrounding pasture and ample views east and west as well as south. It was covered with juniper, brush, and bushes, with a few patches of open meadow interspersed. The driveway was only a short distance from the dirt town road, which is well plowed in winter. Electricity and telephone were connected underground from the road.

The town road bounds the pasture to the north and thus lies behind the new house. The old house lies to the north of the road, and from its elevated position looks across the road to the view toward the south (figure 76).

In our early discussions about what form the dwelling should take on this sloping site, we decided that given our increasing age, we should not have very many steps up and down in our living place. Hence it seemed natural that the house run horizontally on the hillside. This is contrary to the conception in a much earlier sketch I had made when I was younger, which had the house running long in the uphill–downhill direction (figure 75). Nevertheless, in the interest of having the house be a part of the site, we still wanted to incorporate some sense of the slope of the hill. In time the plan developed into two long, level terraces placed some two and a half feet apart vertically (figure 77). Each terrace needed a retaining wall on its uphill side to hold back the earth. These retaining walls contributed the first step in developing the containment that the house would eventually provide.

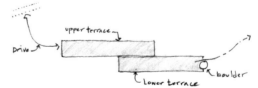

77 Early diagram of upper and lower terraces, driveway, and path to the old house

With these terraces roughly sized and located, I began to think about how the house might be roofed. A low, sloping roof at approximately the same pitch as the slope of the hillside would do much to join these two levels of terraces and reinforce the sense of slope, as shown in the first sketch. (An early diagram of roof framing can be seen in section in figure 78.)

78 Section through the site, showing terracing and possible sloped roof

Then came the issue of the location of the principal places of the house, which would need to find their own positions on these two terraces. The location of the principal place starts somewhere in the middle with an approximate square for the living-dining-kitchen area. There were several conditions on the placement of this space, and it therefore had a primacy over others as to its location. First, it needed to be on the southern terrace, both to take advantage of the view a southern exposure would afford and to permit the passive solar intake of low winter sun (figure 79).

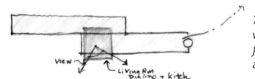

79 Living room situated where two terraces touch, facing south for the view and solar heat

It would be the biggest space in the house, because of its centrality and importance to the whole, and therefore we wanted it to have a greater height than the other spaces and to include both terraces in its extent (figure 78). If we could enter the living space from the upper level, we would have an excellent entry and oversight of the room below and the sense of the descending hillside beyond the room before we descended into it.

The driveway could readily approach the terraces only from the west side of the house, because of the shape of the land and the location of the road. Thus, the driveway and parking, carport, and principal entry to the house all needed to be to the west of this central living space and therefore on the upper terrace. This would then place the porch, patio, garden, and potting shed on the two terraces to the east side of the house. The terrace plan (figure 79) shows this first pass at positioning these elements. This left us the problem of locating the principal bedroom and the study.

The bedroom's need for the most enclosed, protected, and inturned site led us to the north of the central living space on the upper terrace against the earth-retaining wall that defined the north side of that upper terrace. This seemed to add an intimate sense to the design, with the bedroom lying just off the central living space. In this position, it could be lit by skylight over the bed (windows on the north wall were impossible because of the earth behind it) and by a glass door to the garden to the east, which would bring in the first light of the morning sun — a quality that we have come to enjoy considerably since the house was built and we have lived

in it — and a view in summer out to the flower garden just to the east of the bedroom (figure 80).

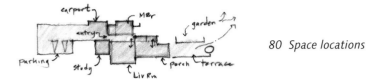

80 Space locations

The study — to be used as a den, a TV room, a guest bedroom, a place to store off-season clothes, and a place for guests to put their coats when they came to dinner — seemed to want to be near the front entry to share the sun and the southern view (figure 80). It is located to the west of the living room and directly off the entry. Figure 81 shows the degree in which the two rectangular terraces shown in figure 77 changed in their plan shape with the actual design of the spaces inhabiting them. A developed plan of the house with a key for locating places in the house is shown in figure 82. A series of photographs of the house, both interior and exterior, with a key will fill out the description of the house (figures 83–87).

81 Terrace plan

How do the themes developed in chapter 1 — trust (attachment, continuity, containment), autonomy, initiative and industry, identity, intimacy and generativity, and loss and restitution — reveal themselves in this work? We will begin with the first three. *Attachments* are in evidence in a number of aspects of this house. The first is the old roots of the locale. Mart's family has owned this old, overgrown, remote pasture for many generations. We can see the roof of Mart's great-grandmother's house on the next ridge, Cleveland Hill. Second, we and our children have made a second home or place here, where we can retreat and renew ourselves away from city life. It has become the psychic home for this family. Partly this is because the place is easy to like. With the pasture cleared, the view is now clear and unobstructed, the pasture is now a field that can be mowed. Part of the old pasture remains covered in low juniper. To us and others the house is both powerful and beautiful. The psychic attachment that we have developed is reinforced by the physical attachment of the house to its surroundings. The house snuggles into the hill, rests along its contours, and is physically embedded in the land as it opens out to nature in the multiple forms of landscape and changing weather, light, wind, animal life, and seasons. It evokes a sense of pleasure as it lies attached to and held by the land.

So that we may be at ease in this somewhat glassy, open "hut in the storm," this array of energy and the size of the surrounding environment need to be offset with sufficient *containment* and sense of shelter. This sense of containment becomes most dear in a driving snowstorm. On clear days it is at once centrifugal and centripetal in a powerful way, outwardly attaching and inwardly abiding in the hearth-centered living space. It is at once warmed and cooled by twentieth-century technology. The house, which is not large — approximately 1,000 square feet — is both heated and cooled by natural processes. In winter the sun does the major heating. The heat from the sun is stored in the masonry floor and fireplace. In summer these masses of masonry stay cool due to the earth's low temperature. A woodstove, set in the masonry mass, supplements the passive solar heating, using a cord of wood each winter. This mix of old and new heating devices achieves an almost constantly sustainable system, one that I am fond of and attached to. One might call this a thermal delight and attachment. Furthermore, in the summer and fall, when the fruits and vegetables from the garden on the east side are harvested, their freshness and availability are a true delight, attaching us at those moments most directly to right here and right now! We are not only attached to this place; we are also eating it, and in that sense we become it!

Containment occurs in a number of dimensions and ways on this sloping pasture, and in and about the house. The plants in the pasture surrounding the house and the hill rising slowly behind it provide a natural sense of containment for the house (and those in it). The first and most immediate level of containment comes from the low grasses and wildflowers that surround our legs as we step from the terrace and move along the path toward the old house. Beyond that, beautiful patches of meadow, flowing each into the next, are edged and defined by juniper, ranging from three to five feet in height and covering perhaps half of the upper pasture as we look south from the house. The junipers provide a second level of containment, and a third level evolves from a more man-made kind of boundary: the stone walls that run horizontally east and west across the field. Beyond those walls, a forest of evergreens — fir, hemlock, and an occasional small pine — provides another level of containment; and this is followed by the next hill, three quarters of a mile away; and then beyond that, the Ossipee and Belknap Mountains, containing the place at a distance. The pleasure afforded by this more remote containment is greatly enhanced by the plurality of the closer ones — the grasses and wildflowers, the juniper-edged meadow, and the firs and hemlocks of varying size. They are smaller than the hills and mountains in the distance, but

82 *Developed plan of house:*

1 Living room
2 Kitchen
3 Porch
4 Garden terrace
5 Path to old house
6 Entry
7 Study
8 Bath
9 Bedroom
10 Storeroom
11 Carport, wood storage

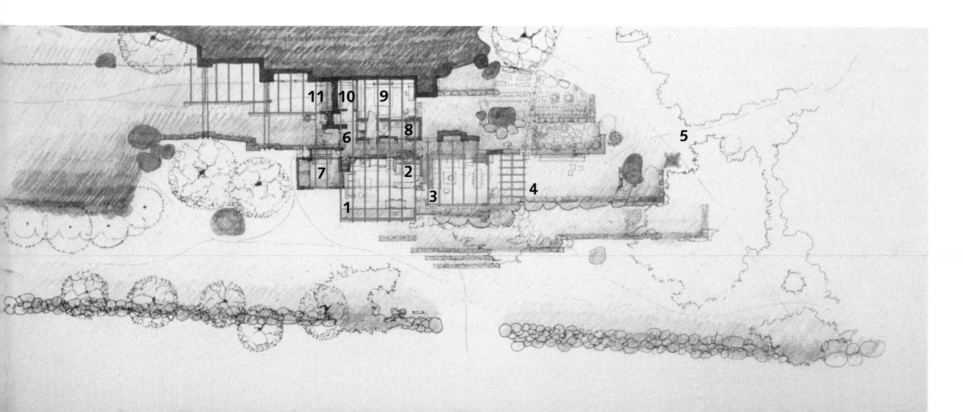

83 *Living room, looking at fireplace on north side of room*

84 *Dining area on the south side of the living room*

they are also closer, and the reassurance we feel from their close-ness provides just as much a sense of containment as the more imposing physicality of the features farther away. In the other direction, behind the house, the upward slope of the hill is the source of another sense of containment: the hillside contains us to the north in a different (but equally important) way from the expanses of meadow and forest to the south.

As we approach the Pasture House from the north returning on the path from the old house, we first come to a boulder at the end of the terrace and a two-foot-high retaining wall that supports the flower garden. We enter through the narrows between the retain-ing wall and the boulder and find the terrace, which is bordered by the wall, the garden, and the hill to the north and the house with its overhanging roof to the west, and uncontained and open to the broad view of Cleveland Hill and the Ossipee Mountains to the south. The sense of close containment provided by the hill and re-taining wall to the north and the contours of the house itself to the west is striking in its contrast to the lack of near containment in the southerly direction, where our eyes must travel a considerable way before meeting a comparable sense of containment in the distant Ossipees.

Other parts of the house structure provide containment in smaller but no less important ways. The back wall of the house is of thick concrete with embedded boulders; similar walls serve as the back wall of the carport and porch and also bound the terrace garden on its north side. These walls, with their feet embedded in the earth and holding back the earth of the hill rising behind, are inextricably engaged with the earth. Through these walls — the initial defini-tions of our place here — we also feel engaged with the earth. In

this way we become attached to the earth and to the beginnings of the place. They also contain the space we are in and thereby contain us.

The wooden structural members that support the roof of the main living space bend as they turn to take the position of the sloped rafters. They do much to give a sense of our being contained in the presence of the great space of the view to the south and east that the living space affords beyond the broad, cushioned seat and

51

85 *Dining area on the east side of the porch*

86 *The Pasture House in winter, viewed from the road*

expanses of glass on the room's southern and eastern walls. Those expanses of glass provide another means of containment, albeit of a rather different type. Low-E film on the glass enables it to contain three quarters of the infrared radiation that it subtends. This radiation is then stored in various passive solar reservoirs provided by the concrete of the room's floor and the masonry of the massive concrete fireplace on the room's north wall. By receiving the light and heat of the sun, by largely containing it through the low-E film on the glass, and by storing it in the passive reservoirs, the house is able to "contain" the sun (or, more exactly, the sun's energy). This containment is a great and a friendly one, as it keeps us warm in the house even during the coldest months.

The highest point of the living room, the peak of the roof, lets in light that balances the light from the south windows. In its geometry, the room is a square, which suggests a stable space, for staying or for remaining. It is not the shape of a long rectangle, which implies directions, as would a corridor or a street; rather, it is inert in this directional sense. With the main bedroom illuminated by skylight and set in against the hill, with only a small face to the east and the morning sun, the sense of the whole house is one of containment, of intimacy, and of being safely backed into the hill, down which it also steps. This containment by the hillside seems to be one of the most important architectural aspects of containment that the house offers. That vast presence — the earth itself — is containing us here.

Finally, in this place of much containment, there is another architectural theme: a series of repeated containments throughout the house, in many forms, where we store artifacts that are valuable to us. There are niches in all directions: shelving for art books, photo albums, a couple of small places in the fireplace mass where many small things are kept, and an ancient family embroidery listing earlier generations of the family. Our food and utensils are stored in the kitchen work area both on exposed shelves and in enclosed cabinets; our clothes are stored in closets, drawers, and cabinets beautifully made from rift-grain firs. All these speak of containment.

The *continuity* the Pasture House offers is not of the same vernacular as that of several old New England farm buildings within sight. Although we love these old houses and would not mind living in one (for they are beautiful and deeply moving), our goal in building this new one has been to explore how we might appropriately evolve our habitat as contemporary occupants of the New England landscape. Our primary sources of food, clothing, and income derive from elsewhere; therefore, we do not seek to demonstrate to God our harmonious intent and thereby ensure our successful crops, as did our forebears who built and occupied the beautiful surrounding farmhouses.

Nor is our house a Thoreau-type house. We do not seek to live as campers, or at subsistence level, or to use only what we can individually make ourselves. We will use happily the most advanced of appropriate technologies such as insulation and the double glazing of the windows with low-E film. Our connection to the land and nature is one we relate to in a broader and less immediate way. We find the land and nature beautiful and deeply meaningful. We understand that we are a part of this nature. We understand that it is not a we/they relationship, but rather a we/we relationship, although we have some considerable learning to do about this. We hope that this house offers a sustainable way of life for ourselves and our offspring. For example, we hope that global warming does not end life as we have known it, or end it entirely, or that the conflicts that will occur from the population expansion will cause a similar difficulty. We would like to live with the nature surrounding the Pasture House in as connecting and harmonious a way as possible, because this house is *us*. If we are to increase our understanding and connection to it, then we will need to exist with it as continuously as possible. In the house and its surroundings, we seek a sense of oneness with the earth and its flora and fauna, with its weather, with its cold and heat, the sense that the infant seeks at birth, a sense of oneness with mother, the achieving of a continuity with her. Just as the infant experiences early life, this will no doubt involve conflicts. Our desire to have bird feeders brings bears, who come for the good-smelling bird seed; the bears are wonderful but they knock down and destroy the feeders, which we then have to replace. Our garden is occasionally visited by rabbits, and I find myself becoming "Mr. McGregor" in defense of the garden, using a homemade trap and transporting the catch across the river. This desire for harmony and continuity with nature is not unlike the harmony with nature that Wright sought, and wonderfully achieved, in the design of Falling Water. The Pasture House was built for a different client, on a different site, with a different budget, and by a different architect, but I think it was a somewhat similar endeavor.

Autonomy is evident in the Pasture House and its surroundings in a subtle way that has to do with its identity. One may ask, How can a thing that has such continuity with all that is around it be autonomous at the same time? If the house is contained by the earth, for example, how is it not a prisoner? The answer can be found in the analogy of a person who is an important part of a neighborhood, continuous with it, respected and loved by its members for these connections, and yet is recognized for his capacity to come to his own conclusions about all sorts of issues, even if some are in conflict with those around him. In him is the combined capacity to be his own man while still part of a larger order. In this sense, the house is integrated with the landscape it inhabits, while preserving an independent identity as one of the centers of the larger landscape surrounding it.

In chapter 1 we discussed *initiative, industry,* and *identity.* In these ages came the decision of the child, with his emerging sense of self, to join his or her family and the greater society of school and other activities, to take initiative, to be industrious, to gain competence, and in time to become a young adult with his own identity. Places go through a similar process. All places have beginnings, originally in nature, with flora and fauna put to use by itinerant hunters and gatherers in creating various forms of portable shelter, such as tents. Many of these natural places were overtaken by agrarians/hunters and gatherers, who in time developed open fields and with this fixed source of food for themselves and their animals began also to build permanent shelters for the protection of harvest, crops, and

87 *The Pasture House in the late fall, hunkered down under the hill*

animals, as well as themselves. With this stability came the first places importantly altered by humans from their natural beginnings. From that point not only did places emerge as farms with buildings, but also clusters of them began to form as villages, towns, and eventually cities. Places at each of the levels of development had their own capacity to offer shelter, food, sociability, defense, and so on — a level of competence in the offering of services that was matched with their inhabitants' own competence to understand the use of such places. Our current urban and suburban places may serve us in a broad range of ways; to understand and make use of this involves a considerable amount of learning about the offerings of a particular place and therefore our expectations of it. In a sense, places have a varied set of competence in their offerings, and we have varied degrees of competence in making use of them. We feel most at ease when our own competence to make use of a place is a good match with the competence of the place to make the expected offering. We feel discomfort when we cannot understand what the place offers us and what it does not offer us.

On the way to fully achieving its emerging identity, the Pasture House went through a series of steps that importantly affected its competence. We made many changes as we began to use the house. We added sun screens for summer, a screened porch, a garden shed, and a barn that consisted of a workshop, an office/guest room, a storeroom, and a sauna. In these ways (and some lesser ways not mentioned), our habitat gained a competence for this period of our lives.

Along with the competence it has developed, the Pasture House has an *identity*. It is a contemporary house unlike others around it. It rests snuggled into the hillside pasture and overlooks a magnficent view. Its form and character, along with the surrounding buildings,

53

have grown out of its sustainability and its attachment and containment with the earth. For its inhabitants it is a continuation of that which went before, but it has found its own independent voice and form, its own identity (figures 86 and 87).

To understand the *generative* aspects of this house, this place, we must think about it in several ways. It is certainly a place that reinforces the sense of a strong and loved family seat for a generation who will spend important amounts of time living elsewhere. It is a place whose habitations can be enlarged considerably over its two hundred acres by subsequent generations, if they are so minded. Further, it is a fixed place of ongoing values that seem particular to this family. A place once occupied by farmers in the family, it has become one that several subsequent generations have returned to for renewal and reconnection to self, family, and extended nature, as the urban nomads that they have become. And the farming itself continues in a modified way.

It is a piece of architecture and landscape architecture that has its own generativity. To us, its generativity seems to lie primarily in the continuity it seeks to establish in the many ways we have described earlier. It is a continuity that sees us as a part of nature, with hopes that it is sustainable in ways that permit us to be sustainable. Further, since we cannot divorce ourselves from our involvement with nature, we would like it to be as harmonious and delightful an existence as possible. This continuity is not an easy one for us to grasp. As a culture, we are used to seeing nature and ourselves as two different things, but we are not. Even in our dense cities and suburbs, we are inseparable from it. In cities, nature is just more densely filled with the human part of nature. Here in North Sandwich, in a nature of relatively low human density, we have sought to use our skills as habitat makers to evolve the sense that we are living more "on a hillside" than "in a house." Even at the center of the house, we are largely connected to the outside without feeling inadequately contained. In the progression from the center of the house outward, there is no sharp discontinuity, but rather an increasing and smooth progression to openness, to the rest of nature (figures 86 and 87).

We come from the dichotomous past of man and nature. The old habits of that understanding have not been easy to overcome. Thus, this habitat is also a heuristic one, one in which we and it can learn about our being cousins who do not always agree or get on well with each other but are a part of each other nonetheless. This probably means we will need to keep some kind of diary to note the progression of our relationship.

Two Dormitories

Our work on student dormitories at two different colleges in the Northeast (figures 93 and 94) was done by my architectural firm Arrowstreet Inc.[26] We'll present these projects together, because they occurred within the same time frame and shared building systems and design goals.

The process began in 1967 when the trustees of what would be Hampshire College asked us to think about what student housing should be like in the experimental college that was being planned. This challenge very much matched our interests. Soon after, the Massachusetts State College Building Authority requested help with student housing problems at Worcester State College. Worcester State needed new housing, but before building anything, the administration needed to know why students were typically trashing their dorms. The authority came to us because it believed that we could answer that question, make a proper program for the space needs of the new buildings, and then design the buildings. The design development for this second project ended up preceding that for Hampshire, so we will begin by discussing Worcester State College.

Our first step was to explore the existing state of student dormitories. We sent one of our student employees with a camera and a tape recorder to research life in the northeastern colleges. He came back with evidence of something on the order of seventeen different dormitory lifestyles. They ranged from a student living all alone in his rented room off campus, to living groups outside the university who made their own arrangements, to communes or cooperatives, to people living in fraternity houses, to people living in trailers, to people in old farmhouses, to people living on campuses in coed and single-sex dorms. This report's lively description of the current state of conditions was very useful to us in our initial planning and conceptualization of what the new dormitories should be like. It broke open the traditional notion of a student residence.

The Massachusetts State College Building Authority had been building student living spaces on the campuses of Massachusetts state colleges at the lowest possible cost so that as many students as possible could afford to attend those schools. This strategy of building economy had led it to construct straight-in-line buildings of one or more floor levels with double-loaded corridors. It was probably the somewhat barrackslike industrial/military form of these structures that led to the trashing of the dorms in the Vietnam period of student unrest. Yet despite the students' negative reactions to the design scheme and the resulting destructive behavior, the authority needed to continue to carry out its mandate to build student dormitories. It sought direction from us as to design and budget.

It was in this context that we developed a space program that identified the diverse living groups that one might expect to house, based on our work with a number of student consultants from Worcester State. Students were offered a choice of living unit size, ranging from four occupants, to eight, or to even larger groups of eleven and fourteen. We proposed living spaces to accommodate groups in these three size ranges. The groups of four students could be housed in single rooms clustered about an entry and bath, all on the same level. The groups of eight could occupy singles and doubles organized about a living/dining/kitchen area and two baths, the entire area spanning two levels. In some cases the largest groups would require three levels of living space. The spaces housing fourteen students were conceived to serve a living/learning group that might be organized about a particular educational mission — for example, learning and speaking French in the living group. The principal dining was to take place in an existing cafeteria, and lesser meals in the apartment kitchenettes or the coffee shop in the complex. There were a few suites organized for married couples, with bedroom, living room, bath, and kitchenette. Later on, Hampshire added to the program several classrooms, faculty offices, a housemaster's suite, and a commons building with a large dining room, as well as student meeting rooms. (The architectural programming required to turn our visions into reality was a major effort, carried out largely by Gary Hack, a Ph.D. candidate in the Urban Studies Program at Massachusetts Institute of Technology.)

In time our proposed program developed into an architectural design set in wooded sites on the Worcester and Hampshire campuses.

88 Worcester dorms

55

89-90-91 Worcester State College. Most ground-floor spaces are used for classrooms. The basic dwelling unit starts at Level 2, with living room, kitchen, bath, and bedrooms. For most units there is a Level 2 and a Level 3. Level 3 has an upper living room with kitchen, bath, and bedrooms. Level 4 has an upper living room, kitchen, bath, and bedrooms, each with a mezzanine for beds up under the peak of the roof.

92 Footprint, Worcester (above)

93 Worcester dorms (right)

94 *Prescott House dormitories, Hampshire College*

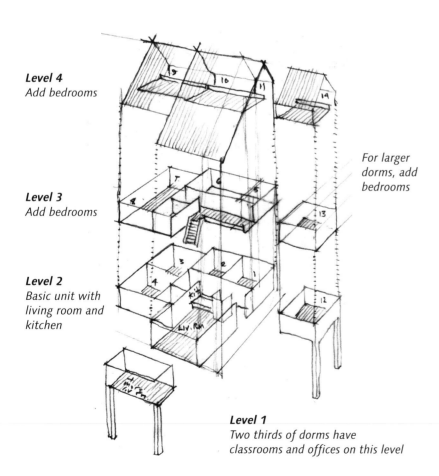

Level 4
Add bedrooms

For larger dorms, add bedrooms

Level 3
Add bedrooms

Level 2
Basic unit with living room and kitchen

Level 1
Two thirds of dorms have classrooms and offices on this level

95 *3-D assembly of the basic units, Worcester State and Hampshire*

Our diverse offerings of different-sized apartment units were orga-nized about a repeating basic pattern of a living-dining-kitchen-bath that looked inward toward a communal area shared by a number of such living spaces. Here we drew on a form we had long admired, the European medieval street or plaza (see again figure 10). In Wor-cester it was a village street (figure 92), in Hampshire a village plaza (figure 98). Each of the common living areas had four student living spaces in the form of singles and doubles (figures 89–91). This foot-print could be expanded upward, giving a two-story living room and four more student living spaces for a suite of eight. Or it could be further expanded upward under a pitched roof for a unit of eleven. As a suite grew in numbers of students, it was possible to add space to it on its outer edges, so that it would be appropriately sized for the number of students it housed. One-, two-, or three-story suites could then be stacked to make a building component of three, four, or five stories (figure 95). This overall design began to suggest small towers of varying height, two of which could be paired about a stair tower to give a basic building increment that could be organized with others in a range of ways about the village street, thus form-ing the principal common space (see figures 96, 97, 99). To this building increment we then added fire escapes, which were placed on the sides of the village street so that they could form useful bal-conies as well off the different levels of living rooms. The common space of the village street, through which all the living spaces were accessed, was envisioned as a place to come and go, to hang out and throw Frisbees and such: a great place to socialize. It would be overhung by all the living rooms and balconies/fire escapes. The central common space would run north and south with the living spaces on each side, so that in the woodland setting of the site, the low-slanting winter sun could fill its long dimension during the middle four or more hours of the day. (See the footprints of the

96 *Village street between dormitories, Hampshire*

97 *Hampshire dormitories*

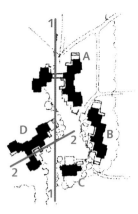

98 *Footprint, Hampshire*

Worcester State and Hampshire projects, figures 92 and 98). The actual dormitory rooms mainly looked outward, away from the common street and into the woods.

The Worcester State project was partly built when the president of Hampshire College decided, after visiting it, that he would like spaces of the same type to accommodate three hundred students, this time with a dining component, to be built at Hampshire in the subsequent twelve months. The college's existing traditional brick dorms did not fit the image it had of itself as an innovative college; things seemed to have gotten off track. The president asked us if we could work on the problem of making an environment in which students would feel more empowered. A similar woodland setting at Hampshire made the Worcester State design a ready fit for Hampshire's needs. In what follows, we will identify the ways in which the themes identified in earlier portions of this book are found in the design of these two student dwelling projects.

There is much of *attachment*, *continuity*, and *containment*, in these spaces. There are two general ways in which a student can experience attachment here. A sense of attachment comes from these dormitories being places where students are empowered in their living and in their work. It also comes more generally from the associative connections that have been included in the design.

Empowerment is embodied in the series of choices the students make in inhabiting the place. Unlike the traditional student housing of the period, which consisted of single and double rooms along a double-loaded corridor, the options in these two dormitories are plural. One can live alone (and there are those who want that), be assigned to groups of different sizes, or live with a student group of choice (or, in the Worcester case, even live in a small apartment designed for married couples). In all of these options, the place a student has for living is a suite of rooms or an apartment, just as she finds in the adult world. Herein lies the great difference between these spaces and traditional dorms: Students at

Worcester State and Hampshire are being treated as young adults, not regimented as if they were not up to living as adults do. Further, the dwellings at Worcester State and Hampshire are organized in such a way that groups could design to some degree their modes of coexisting. For example, kitchen and dining space is included in each living area, but the design also provides for communal eateries such as coffee shops. At Hampshire there is also a dining commons at the south end of the village street. The designers expected that students would usually eat in the commons. As it turned out, the economics of student life and the lifestyles of students were changing, and there was increased pressure for them to cook for themselves and in their own style, which they then increasingly did. It was the time of the greening of America and of doing your own thing! In the period during which the design was conceived and developed, student living was not yet coed, but coed dormitories were thought to be a possibility. By the time the students moved into the freshly built dormitories at Hampshire in 1974, however, it had become the new way. The smaller, more homelike bathrooms of the new dorms seemed to work especially well for coed arrangements compared to the large communal bathrooms of traditional dormitories.

57

99 *Hampshire dormitories*

100   101   102   103

Architectural form references for dormitories: The New England farmhouse and barn and the shed roof of a wilderness shelter led to the pitched roofs of the dorms.

At Hampshire, students in spaces with two-story living rooms were permitted to build platforms of wood frame and planks as part of forming their own place and making more space to live in. Students were also given a kit of furnishing parts so that they could build a personalized "living landscape" in their own rooms. These kits contained simple elements: boxes of two different types (two low ones with drawers for files and clothes and one tall, narrow one for hanging clothes); two flat, doorlike panels (one for a desk and one for a bed); a mattress; and possibly a chair or two. With this combination, a student could live on the floor, Japanese-style, or sleep up near the ceiling with desk and chair at intermediate level, or some other arrangement that suited him better. One possible agenda for spatial organization is to make the small room seem vast by way of Japanese *tatami* mats and plain surfaces. The windows in the buildings ran floor to ceiling, so living at floor level did not seem to cut off anyone from the world outside, as an occupant would feel with the standard windowsills at thirty inches above the floor. The design of these buildings around a common space — including the metal balconies and stairs overhanging the village way — greatly increased the possibility of students socializing and interacting compared to that offered by a traditional arrangement. The village way became, as the designers intended, a place for Frisbees, hanging out, seeing someone you wanted to talk to, or just connecting (figures 88 and 96).

The outer edges of the buildings in these dormitories were very different from those of the brick boxes of previous dorms, which did not invite interaction, as they had no village street defined by dorms on either side. The dorms had ample openings and fire escapes/balconies, so that if a student wanted to socialize, she could hang out in the street or at the edge of her living room/balcony and call down to a passing friend, throw a Frisbee, or whatever. (It is not that the brick dorms didn't have a lot of students, but that it had never been imagined that this kind of communal activity could take place right where the students lived.) We can immediately see how all of these attributes of the new places we designed would be at-

tractive to a student and would offer him a place that he could really live in and become attached to.

An additional set of associations in the work on these dormitory spaces also bears on the issue of attachment. The dorms were conceived and built in a difficult time, during the Vietnam War; the domestic unrest it created was significant, particularly among the age group who would live in the dorms. This was a time when the young came to distrust the old hierarchical ways of seeing and doing things. Were these not the very habits that were sending good mothers' sons to fight a war of dubious justification? It was also a time of seeking old human truths: valuing what it was to be a person, what was commonplace, what were good places, the greening of the country, the empowerment of people. Although the form of the dormitory buildings is somewhat unusual, with their metal roofs and fire escapes on the front, there is nevertheless much that is familiar in the grain of their order. Their metal pitched roofs (figures 99, 103, and 105) are reminiscent not only of the ubiquitous metal-roofed barns, sheds, and farmhouses of New England, but also of the bright frozen ponds of the area's winter landscapes. The fire escapes are painted a deep red at Hampshire and a bright yellow at Worcester State, so they are a more pleasant place to be than the utilitarian black fire escapes that we know: a positive, rather than a negative, element in the buildings' composition. As such they add a vibrant, enriching layer to the elevations. There is another set of associations to these fire escapes and metal roofs: that of the industrial vocabulary. There is a kind of straightforward toughness about how things are organized and built — a welcome straightforwardness, it seemed to us, in a period when little else seemed straight (see figures 104–107).

Containment occurs in these dormitory buildings in several ways and levels of size. First, it occurs in the apartment-like quarters they offer, akin to the familiar containment that we are used to in our homes and apartments. Coed groups in single and double rooms, living rooms, kitchens, and bathrooms sufficiently contained them

58

104   105   106   107

Another architectural form reference: The straightforwardness of the Pittsburgh steel mills suggested clarity and straightness at a time of cultural confusion.

privately and communally in ways that are largely familiar from previous abodes. This atmosphere, and the kind of containment it offers, is very different from that of the barracks-like or long-corridor dormitories.

Second, the various levels of the dwellings, from three to five stories, are approached by means of a village street, which the living rooms overlook. The connection between these upper living rooms and the street below them may be seen in the brightly painted fire escapes that were also used as balconies and in the buildings' stairwells, which offered the inhabitants a pathway to the street. The village street in itself is dominantly and intimately containing, through the massing of dwellings whose height is often greater than the width of the street. Further, the street bends, which helps contain through shortening of the visible length. At the end of each of the two streets, the buildings bridge the street, helping to visually close it at that point (see figure 108).

There is one other important characteristic of this containment, which has to do with the living rooms and fire escapes/balconies fronting on the street. It is not a blank and unseeing wall that is containing the way. Rather, it is a large student population that can see into and across the street, either from the balcony or from the living room. It is a containment by a living and lively population. The effect is somewhat like that found on streets in Boston's North End, with mothers leaning out second-story windows, talking across or down the narrow way to their neighbors, friends, and children. This, too, is a kind of social containment by friends and neighbors (see again figures 88 and 96).

At points, there are openings between the buildings. These openings are filled by the surrounding woods, thus continuing the sense of containment. In good weather, the balconies are occupied, and there is much chance of meeting, catching someone's eye, and other forms of sociability that can come from intimate and contained places. In both the Hampshire and Worcester State configu-

rations, an important part of the village is that it is enclosed by a wood, which adds to this substantial sense of containment, in looking out from the individual rooms and in our general sense of the place when at its center. The whole complex is not on open plain but instead stands in extensive and mature woodland. (Worcester's site is a pine woodland and Hampshire's is deciduous.) The buildings were arranged so that the street between the buildings runs north to south, creating a space bounded by the buildings on two sides that could be "filled" by the low winter sun, thus offering containment of another sort.

There are two important kinds of *continuity* at work in the space created by these buildings. The first is that of the apartment form of abode clustered about a common way and accessed by an entry stair, reflecting the vernacular of the denser living spaces in our towns and cities. This arrangement is akin to the way we ordinarily live as adults in such densities, as opposed to the long corridors and barrackslike quality of the traditional college dorms. It offers an important and much needed continuity for students between the way they live in the rather artificial world of college and the real world they occupied prior to entering college and will occupy again once they leave it. The second kind of continuity lies in the spatial order of the building. This is a lateral continuity offered by a series of vertical elements, a collection of vertical open accesses to the buildings; the narrow village street is framed by the verticality of the buildings that enclose it. Internally, verticality is offered by the two- or three-story living room spaces and the internal stair in the living room that connects one floor to another. This verticality extends into the surrounding woods of the building's context.

A sense of *autonomy* is established in the overall form of the Hampshire project. While the larger order is established by building groups A, B, and C (see again figure 98) — these define axis 1 in the N–S direction — building group D is rotated and defines axis 2 in a NE–SW direction. In addition to providing important containment in the SW direction for the village street, this positioning of building

59

The arrangement of the living quarters in these dormitories, as compared with those in traditional barrackslike dormitories, can reinforce a student's emerging competence by being a competent place for these purposes. The dwelling unit's form creates the capacity both for individual work, in the private space of the room, and for living with others in the social way, in the communal living rooms, dining areas, and balconies. In this sense the dwelling unit has a competence. It can enable the life activities it was intended to enable. Its inhabitants can be industrious and take initiative in ways that are useful to their education. They are not blocked by the absence of this supporting form, as they might be if they were in a "barracks." Thus, the building itself enables students to take initiative and be industrious.

Each of these places, each of these dormitories, has an *identity,* like that of a person who grows up and gains a unique sense of self. They have this identity because the design took into account a student's need for attachment, continuity, and containment, as well as his need for sociability and a place to work and be industrious. All these themes came together to form a place with a unique identity, by offering the students the possibility of many different lifestyles, ranging from solo individuals to large groups forming a social living situation together, with a number of possibilities in between. The identity of this place is not the identity of the "brick dorm." Rather, it is an identity that speaks to and addresses the new needs of these young people at the time in their lives when they occupy it.

Any discussion of the identity of habitats such as dormitories needs to consider the many private bedroom and communal spaces that make them up. The way that they are sized, furnished, distributed, and related one to another is key to sensing the place. This identity may occur at four different levels: first, the student room; second, the apartment; third, the building block (here the building block may vary from three to five stories, with the higher ones accompanied by a stairwell block); and fourth, the communal place (either a village way, as at Worcester, or a village plaza, as at Hampshire).

We have discussed the student room, and in particular how the students at Hampshire could build their own roomscape from a premade kit of parts. This is a particularly interesting approach in that it empowered a student to be creative and give the space

PERSPECTIVE LOOKING SOUTHWEST

108 Perspective view of Worcester, showing dorm layout and village street

group D expresses an independence or autonomy from the larger and therefore dominant massing of building groups A, B, and C. The net result of the overall form at Hampshire is to suggest a dominant order (the N–S village way), which is clear and reassuring, in dynamic harmony with elements of some independence from the dominant order. This is not a bad context for young people to grow in.

In the case of these dormitories, a suitable competence of the place would seem to depend on three conditions. First, that the student feel empowered by the place, that he perceive it as a good place to be, one that reinforces him with respect to his purposes for being there. The place is understandable; he can feel oriented there, that it is vivid, interesting, and alive. Second, that the place permit him to study in quiet and focused comfort in his single or shared room for substantial periods of time. And third, that it permit another central activity of college life — socializing with others: in discussion of the issues of the moment, in cooking and eating in a sociable context, in sports, in dating, in free time, or in some combination of these.

something of his own identity (or, in the case of a double, the combined identities of the students occupying it). The apartment living-kitchen-dining spaces could also take on some identity from the groups that occupied them in terms of their cuisine and wall hangings placed there, and, at Hampshire, the furnishings the groups were permitted to build for the spaces they occupied.

At the level of the tower of apartments, the living rooms of each apartment look out on the village way or plaza, and most of the bedrooms (singles and doubles) look out in the opposite direction to the woods that surround both of the dormitory developments. The orientation of the private rooms, away from the interest of the comings and goings and other social activities of the village street or plaza and into the trees of the woods, seemed a good way to provide a context for privacy and the concentration needed for study. In this sense, the public orientation on one side and the private orientation on the other is an important characteristic of the dormitory's overall identity.

Two apartment towers on either side typically share a central stairwell and a fire escape on the village way side of the tower. The stairwell is seen as not only a fire escape but also as a balcony where a student can hang out. It was also a way to move directly from an apartment living room down to the communal way or the reverse. Thus the community space of the apartment is connected directly to the village way by both the fire escapes and the stair tower and also by eyesight from the living room windows to the street below.

This may seem like a spatial description, and of course it is, but it is also key to the spatial identity of the place. It identifies the range of needed occupancies, from those that require privacy, such as sleep and work, to the apartment communal space, to the larger village communal space. The three- to five-story height establishes a sufficient density for college life as well as efficient land use. With this density there is access to a range of social options, from the privacy of the single room all the way to the social opportunities of the three-hundred- or five-hundred-person community. Both of these options and all the ones in between are important to the purpose of such habitation, in providing the inhabitants with the capacity to select their preference at any time.

The outer crust of rooms, facing the woods, is like a beehive. If beehives had communal rooms, there would be an inner layer of larger hivelike spaces with connections out or down to the communal way that we humans seem to need for movement and sociability. When the towers of habitation are considered together, they form a larger order of building walls that lie between the woods and the communal way or center. The outer edge of the building wall is where most of the private rooms (both singles and doubles) are located, facing toward the woods. The inner edge of the building wall, facing the communal way, is made up of living/dining rooms. These two layers of living space, one facing out, the other in, are intimately connected in each dwelling unit. The building walls are regularly interrupted by entry stairways, and sometimes by gaps between buildings (occasioned by changes in direction), or by access ways needed to provide a means of passage through a building.

The sixth and seventh ages, of *intimacy* and *generativity,* may influence our work in several ways. Perhaps the most important of these is that they draw us to places in our lives that have enough richness, identity, and intensity that members of the next generation understand the incredible importance of place to us. They continue to shape and use these places in their own lives and thereby extend their use to another generation. This generation may revere the past by making it part of themselves. As we have said, this does not mean that they must copy it. With this understanding they are capable of making their own present, including innovation, and looking to the future. The form of places needs to be economically adaptable to future residents, so that incremental change can occur as needed over time without loss of deeper identity. Finally, generations of place makers may have a recognizable imprint that they impose on a place, a DNA of spatial order, establishing a meaningful continuity over considerable time. For example, the underlying continuity of our agrarian past has carried with it a deep imprint over great stretches of time, establishing one of our most meaningful continuities. The farmer's tradition of creating a harmonious continuity throughout all portions of his farmstead, but particularly in the marrying of farmhouse and land, has been imprinted and handed down from one generation to the next for many generations.

We wanted to give the forms of these two residences enough richness, identity, and intensity of our own times to serve as a reference for such qualities of place for future generations. We also thought the forms were capable of change. No one aspect of the design of the residences was absolutely fixed in our thought about the form: If we paid attention to its underlying spirit, or identity, we could contemplate considerable change in response to as yet unknown needs of the place. And given enough change, even the underlying identity could change in positive ways. The approximate model on which it was more or less based — that of a medieval village way with its lateral continuities — can permit much change without loss of its underlying continuity.

Two Urban Design Projects

Our third and last exploration is two linked urban design projects at the city scale, as shown in figures 109 and 109a. The first project is the Government Center design for Boston. It was done in 1959–60 by Fred Adams, Lawrence Anderson, Kevin Lynch, Hideo Sasaki, and others, with myself as chief designer and head of the project staff. The Boston Planning Board acted as our client. The second project is the downtown Boston waterfront, immediately adjacent to the east; it followed three years later (1962–63). This project was done by Kevin Lynch, myself, and Sy Mintz acting as administrator of the project. It was funded by the Greater Boston Chamber of Commerce with the Boston Redevelopment Authority, headed by Ed Logue, acting as client for the city. It comprised the area of Faneuil Hall, Quincy Market, and the ancient Blackstone block.

Boston's Government Center

As of the late 1950s, the city of Boston had built almost nothing since the 1920s, because of the Depression, the Second World War, and inner-city conflicts. There was a concern that spread of the honky-tonk of Scollay Square and the rundown old fabric north of State Street would threaten any future expansion of State Street and the Central Business District (CBD). The city was in need of a new city hall of some half a million square feet and a new federal building of possibly one million square feet. In addition, there was a great need for expansion of private office space. It was thought that an urban renewal project in this area just north of State Street, funded in part by the new Federal Urban Renewal Program, might do much to answer these needs.

The proposed location for this urban renewal project was a key place in the topography of the city (figure 109). The nose of Beacon Hill and the historic cove of the Old Harbor, centered on what is now called Quincy Market, lie on a common axis and are fairly close to one another. The distance from what is now called Cambridge Street (about halfway up Beacon Hill) to the edge of the original cove is approximately 1,000 feet, a small dimension at city scale. However, the juxtaposition of the hill and the cove (figure 110) was not recognizable at this point for several reasons. First, the cove had been filled in, so it no longer existed as a cove. Second, the building of access ramps to the Central Artery (an elevated highway running through the city) had closed off the common axis, so there was no sense of connection between Quincy Market and the harbor. Third, even if we could see or travel along this axis, the waterfront area had decayed to such a degree that it was difficult to get to the water itself or even to *want* to be there (figure 109a). Over time, this connection would become an important element of our design. Not only was it important to remake such a connection for purposes of orientation (our sense of our connection to the sea having been cut off), but other matters were also essential, in terms of urban form, in regenerating the connection. It was viewed as necessary for our ability to connect such significant elements of Boston's physiognomy — Beacon Hill and Boston Harbor. This was of profound significance in how we orient ourselves and understand and use the city. In addition, sensing the highest point of the city (Beacon Hill summit) and the lowest (the harbor), and their close reciprocal juxtaposition, was a significant aspect of the urban form (figure 110).

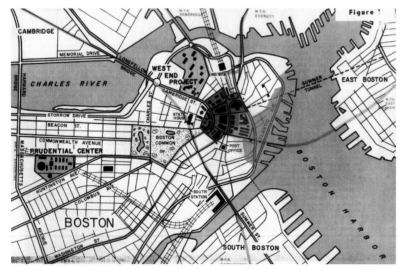

109 Proposed locations of two linked projects. The red-tinted area indicates Boston's Government Center; the blue-tinted area indicates the waterfront.

109a Boston from above: Beacon Hill at the top (1), Government Center midway down in elevation (2), and the waterfront in the foreground (3)

Beacon Hill

Boston Harbor

110 Diagrammatic section showing Beacon Hill, where the highest point in Boston is next to the lowest

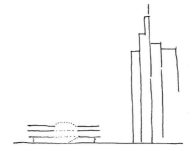

113 City Hall was planned to be low — a foreground building — its horizontality contrasting with the CBD's vertical towers.

Although preservation was not a central theme in this first project, it seemed mandatory to preserve three particular elements of the built landscape, for both architectural and historic reasons: Faneuil Hall, Quincy Market, and the Blackstone block, which preserved the original street pattern of the city. The fine-grained fabric of blocks and streets of the central project area was not capable of accepting the placement of the new city hall, with its architectural program of half a million square feet. It was too big a building to fit into one or even a number of the old small blocks, let alone add a federal building of one million square feet. The solution was to undertake clearance of the fine-grained streets and blocks to make room for these much larger buildings (figure 111).

This found the city hall's horizontal, accessible form contrasting with the vertical towers of the Central Business District (figure 113), and its location (then above Faneuil Hall and across Congress Street from it) fronting a not-too-large uphill plaza as a fore space for the building itself and a place for public events (figure 114).

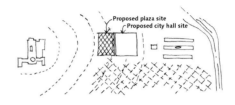

114 A government center plaza was proposed on the uphill side of City Hall.

111 This drawing shows both the fine-grained existing fabric and the key buildings to be preserved: Faneuil Hall, Quincy Market, and the Blackstone Street block — the only remaining original street pattern of the city.

Locating the city hall and determining its general form were important steps, but there still remained much work in locating the federal building and private office buildings. First, we needed to develop a system of new streets, which in time evolved into a circumferential and radial pattern in match with the form of the existing topography and the existing street pattern surrounding the project area (figure 115). We then developed a system of spatial order of building masses and open space (figure 116). In turn this led to a scheme of

63

The next major task was to find an appropriate location and form for City Hall. A number of possibilities were considered within the project area. Two extremes that I particularly recall were a high-rise tower set as far up on Beacon Hill as possible (that is, above and west of Cambridge Street) and a low, open, and accessible building to avoid as much as possible the Kafkaesque image of the remote, inaccessible, and unresponsive bureaucracies of an ever-expanding government. In this second scheme, the building was to be set on mid-hillside, so that it would give the sense of being part of the city's daily business and not attempting to compete with the State House, a competition it could not hope to win. We decided, in time, on the latter of these two alternatives (figure 112).

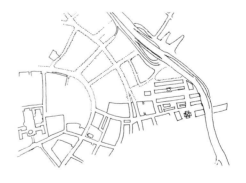

115 Next, develop a street system in a circumferential/ radial pattern to match the topography, the traffic desire lines, and the radial connection to the Harbor and the Sea.

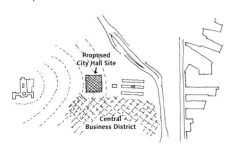

112 Proposed seat of city decision making, on the flank of the hill adjacent to the Central Business District (CBD)

116 Proposed street pattern with buildings to be preserved:

1. Faneuil Hall
2. Quincy Market
3. Blackstone Street block

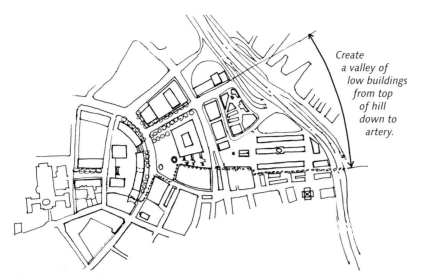

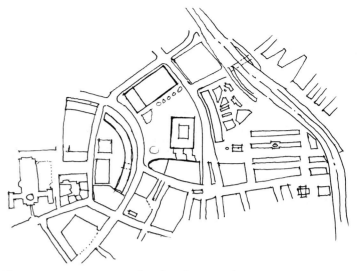

*Create
a valley of
low buildings
from top
of hill
down to
artery.*

117 *Deploy buildings whose massings are in match with the proposed circumferential/radial grid developed in figure 115.*

118 *I. M. Pei's revisions to the plan shown in figure 117. Note the vast increase in the size of the space in which City Hall sits.*

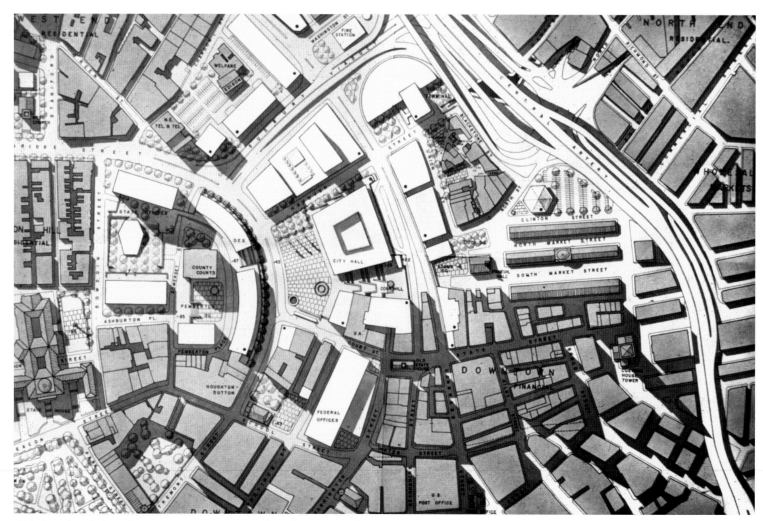

119 *Developed plan of Government Center, 1960, by Adams, Howard and Greeley with Lawrence Anderson, Hideo Sasaki, Kevin Lynch, and John Myer*

overall massing (figure 117). Within this general scheme lay the beginnings of what was to become "the walk to the sea" — a walk from the State House through the new Government Center project area across two ramps of the Central Artery at the east end of the Quincy Market and ending at the water's edge. This aspect of the plan would eventually lead to the removal of these two blocking ramps, thereby reinforcing the connection between Beacon Hill and the harbor. All of these considerations came together in an overall plan (see figure 126).

Shortly after the planning board accepted this general plan, John Collins was elected mayor; he appointed Edward Logue as head of the newly combined Boston Redevelopment Authority and Boston Planning Board (generally known as the BRA). Logue's arrival prompted a whole series of renewal projects funded primarily by the Federal Urban Renewal Program, including a neighborhood renewal plan for the area from State Street to the North Station. I. M. Pei was brought in to carry out this project, which included the Government Center project. While the work of Pei's design accepted many of our previous ideas, including the general positioning of City Hall, much of the detail was changed. The plaza in front of and to the north of City Hall became vast and uncontained (figure 118) as compared to that proposed in our plan (figures 117 and 119), a condition that as yet has not been resolved.

The Waterfront

During this period, the business interests of the city's Central Business District (CBD) were pressing the BRA to undertake an urban renewal project for the greatly decayed downtown waterfront. Money for the city's share of the funding of this project was not then available. Therefore, it was agreed that the Greater Boston Chamber of Commerce would fund its initial planning stages. The chamber of commerce in turn selected Sy Mintz, Kevin Lynch, and John Myer as a team to carry out the initial stages of planning, such as coming up with an overall scheme for the extent of the project (figures 109 and 120). The scheme was to address the serious decay existing in the waterfront area (figure 121). Unlike the Government Center project and despite the decay, there was much that warranted preservation here and, in fact, much has been preserved (figure 122).

The decay of Boston's downtown waterfront had a number of causes. Key among them was the revision of rail rates in 1911, which shifted the economy of transportation southward from Boston's port to New York, Philadelphia, and Baltimore. Although there was still some shipping activity at the downtown waterfront in the early 1930s, the Depression and the Second World War led to an eventual abandonment of the waterfront. There remained a series of

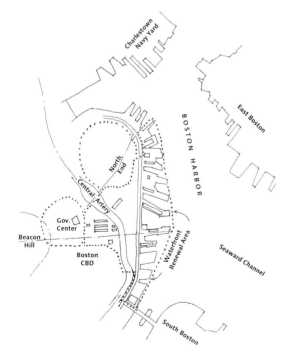

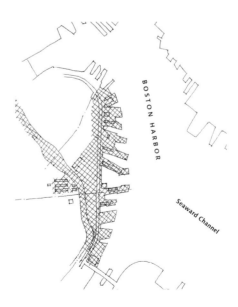

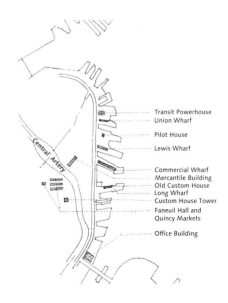

120 Topography, existing conditions, and project boundaries of the Boston Downtown Waterfront Plan, 1962

121 Decay of waterfront (indicated by crosshatching), 1962

122 Proposed conservation of existing buildings

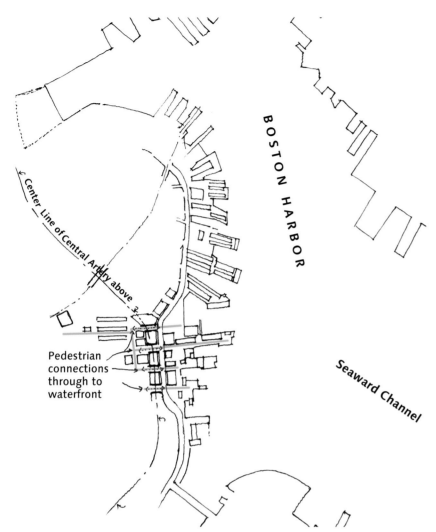

BOSTON HARBOR

Seaward Channel

← Center Line of Central Artery above

Pedestrian
connections
through to
waterfront

123 Reconnect Boston to the harbor and the sea, including the completion of the "walk to the sea."

small fish markets along Atlantic Avenue, a number of decaying buildings, and extensive parking for the CBD on the unused wharves. A number of wharves were collapsing. The barrier-like character of the Central Artery presented an obstacle for any renewal efforts. It would be difficult for the real estate strength of the inland side of the artery to extend past this barrier and form new growth on the waterside. Over time, with the help of many consultants, an overall renewal scheme emerged to include the following elements: the removal of the barrier effect of the Central Artery; the removal of decay; the introduction of new uses to the area (such as CBD and regional uses); and the introduction of functions that would draw business and recreation — office space, a hotel, residential buildings, retail shops, restaurants and bars, marine recreation and transport, an aquarium, parks, and marinas (figure 123).

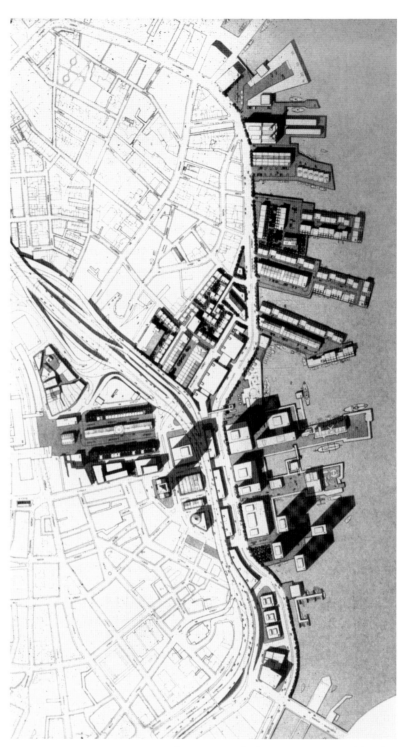

124 Boston's Downtown Waterfront Renewal Plan, 1963. Prepared for the Boston Redevelopment Authority, funded by the GBCC. Planners and architects: Kevin Lynch, John Myer, and Sy Mintz

The issue of reducing the barrier effect of the Central Artery was of primary concern, and it proved difficult to solve. Because of its importance to the overall design, we will discuss our solution briefly.

As we considered the two alternatives that we perceived as being available to us (suppressing the artery underground, which seemed far too expensive and disruptive, or leaving it above grade), it occurred to us that if we could remove the dark, noisy street under the artery and build commercial space under the artery structure itself that would front on the streets and ways crossing under it, we would have overcome the worst part of the barrier effect: the dark, noisy, under-artery street. It was a solution at a much lower cost than any other available. It would have an added benefit: The roofed portion of this crossing street would act as a portico to the waterfront with suitable architecture to make it an attractive one (figure 123). Although the idea did not comply with Department of Transportation guidelines (the DOT funded and owned the highway and did not want buildings under its major highways), we hoped the department might come to see that the benefits we envisioned were worth struggling with, not only here but also in the many places where major highways disrupt the urban fabric. Today, a scheme along the same lines might have saved the city, state, and federal government considerable sums of money, and degrees of dislocation in the downtown highway project (referred to as the "Big Dig") that Boston has been suffering.

The final overall scheme (figures 124 and 126) was to include the removal of the old railway on Atlantic Avenue and a relocation inland by a block of the central portion of Atlantic Avenue itself. This would permit us to arrange a pedestrian zone at the center of the Boston downtown waterfront where the old cove had existed, and then to place in this zone a park, a hotel, an aquarium, housing, parking, wharves for ferries and tour boats, and a public open space at the end of Long Wharf where one could visit the harbor space itself. The park and the other pedestrian areas would become the arrival point on the waterfront for "the walk to the sea" mentioned above. On the north side of this central district, the future development of the waterfront project was to involve primarily housing. To the south it was to incorporate a major development with a hotel, office space, more housing, and a terminal for a ferry to cross the harbor to the airport, as well as the renewal of an old office building for the use of the federal government.

In what follows, we will attempt to identify how the ideas developed in previous chapters find themselves in these two projects. The possibilities for *attachment* to this area of Boston are multiple, for at the time of the beginning of these two projects, it was a place with excellent potential for becoming a rich and wonderful area imbued with a great sense of history (though largely abandoned and in disrepair at the time):

- *The east edge of Beacon Hill*, close to Boston's deep old harbor
- *State House*, with its handsome architecture and glittering dome
- *Faneuil Hall* at the bottom
- *Quincy Market*
- *Blackstone block* (the only original street pattern and buildings)
- *Union Oyster House*
- *State Street* itself
- *Old State House*
- *The North End*, and the granite warehouses on the waterfront

We immediately feel connected and attached to these buildings and places. There is the powerful architecture of both the new and the existing buildings. Our awareness of the significance of the old buildings in the Revolutionary War is still vivid. What a beginning for these two urban renewal projects!

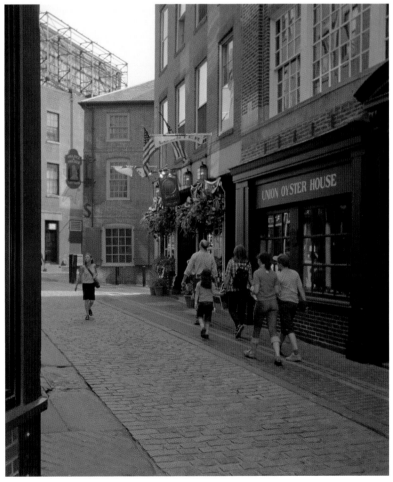

125 *We find the narrow, often winding public ways of the North End, Beacon Hill, and the Central Business District to be an immediate pleasure because we feel contained in an intimate public place . . . one that permits us to feel large and somehow connected to others whom we come across in these ways.*

Like those for attachment, the possibilities for *containment* here are great in both the public and the private spaces of its urban fabric. As most of us are familiar with modern American cities, where much of the modern public ways are straight and broad and part of an easily understood grid system, we find the narrow, often winding ways of the North End, the CBD, Beacon Hill, and the approaches to the waterfront an immediate pleasure. We feel contained in an intimate public place, an unusual experience for us, one that makes us feel large and somehow connected to the others whom we come across in these ways (figure 124). It also reminds us of earlier times and ways of being. In these old ways we are also contained by a sense of the past and of history. It is this sense that we sought to extend into the spaces and buildings of the design of Government Center and the waterfront. This sense of containment does not exist in the current spaces of Government Center about City Hall because our original design was modified by subsequent planners (see again figure 118). This later step in the process generated a place different from the original design, one with no containment, one that offers little opportunity for attachment. In the future, with enough new building in the excess of space in Government Center Plaza, a sense of containment might be returned to the place. Recall the earlier discussion of containment and the great space of the Piazza San Marco and what a delight it is to find containment in that grand, public, purposeful space. The current configuration of Government Center offers us no such sense. However, we do have it in the renewed Quincy Market, and it is a pleasure to be there.

A sense of *continuity* throughout this area is conveyed in several ways. First, there is the containment of the urban fabric, which contains us in both its public and its private spaces. Next, there are the radial and circumferential streets. The radial ones connect the business district to the waterfront and the North End; the circumferential ways connect the CBD and the West End. (The "walk to the sea," which penetrates the Central Artery, uses one of these radials linking the State House to the sea and the hill to the harbor in that reciprocal exchange of mass and void: the mass of the hill juxtaposed to the void of the harbor.) Finally, there is the continuity between the past and the present in the mix of structures and ways that date from a number of previous eras.

One other continuity deserves mention: a micro-continuity compared to those mentioned above. I recall vividly — when I was a young designer working on this project — eating a dozen oysters on the old, curved, cracked, heavy wooden counter in the bay window of the Union Oyster House. The oysters were just opened off the mound

of ice in the middle of the circular counter. I thought it was a terrific old place. I could feel how it used to be and how many of the past generations had done the same thing in this very place. At that moment and locus, the continuity of time and place seemed immediate and very powerful.

The waterfront area also needs to display a sense of *competence* to match our own competence. Although this competence may have multiple specific aspects, it has a few general conditions that we must mention. First, the area needs to be made up of "sub places" to match the diverse and vital activities that it was intended to accommodate. These include business, recreational, residential and governmental activities; markets; and public events and places of entertainment, such as bars, restaurants, parks, and plazas, including water-edge parks. Some of these activities thrive in a mixed-use setting; others do better in a setting designed for a single use.

Second, the area needs to handle various forms of through and local traffic, including that from cars, buses, and trucks (as well as parking for all of these), subways, boats and ferries of many sorts, and particularly a ferry to and from the airport. In all of this, it is essential that the various users of the streets, ways, and places have a sense of being oriented, of knowing where they are and how to get from one place to another. Competence for this area requires that the sub places and the overall place have an identity, that the sub places and the overall place have a particular and understandable sense of self, that they are good and friendly places.

The issue of *identity* for this place, the Government Center/downtown waterfront, needs to be addressed in both spatial and temporal terms. The place is centered on an axis that parallels the "walk to the sea" and starts at the State House (see figure 126): the red line is the walk to the sea; spaces are numbered and buildings are lettered. Let's walk along it and see the major elements.

From the State House (a), we proceed easterly and downhill, passing through Pemberton Square (7), through Government Center Plaza (3), through or by City Hall (b), across Congress Street and past Dock Square (8), Faneuil Hall (d), and the Blackstone block (f) to our left, and through Quincy Market (e) and (9). At the end of the market we take a brief jog to the right to arrive at State Street, where we return to an easterly course at the foot of the Custom House Tower (g) on State Street, making a straight shot through the Portico (10) and the now barely noticeable Central Artery, to cross almost immediately Atlantic Avenue (relocated a block to the west of its former position). Next we arrive at the long-filled Old Harbor

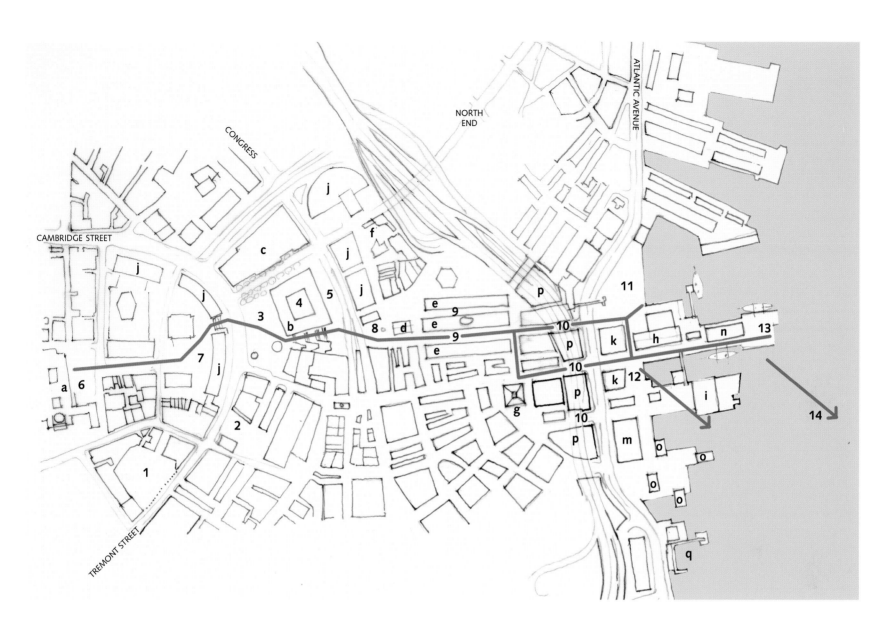

The Walk to the Sea

BUILDINGS

a State House
b New City Hall
c New Federal Building
d Faneuil Hall
e Quincy Market
f Blackstone Street block
g Custom House Tower
h New hotel
i New aquarium
j New office buildings

k Renovated existing old buildings
m Parking garage with commercial ground floor
n Old Custom House
o New apartment towers
p New buildings to be built under the Central Artery
q Marina

SPACES

1 Old Granary Burial Ground
2 Space about King's Chapel
3 New Government Center Plaza
4 Atrium of City Hall
5 Arrival space of City Hall
6 Space flanking the State House
7 Pemberton Square
8 Adams Square

9 Space in Quincy Market
10 Improved crossing under Central Artery
11 Waterfront Park
12 Central space of waterfront
13 End of Long Wharf
14 Seaward direction

126 A space-positive map of the Government Center and the Downtown Waterfront Projects shown together

Cove, which is now a waterfront pedestrian zone (12). The old line of Atlantic Avenue can be seen as straight north and south. (The purpose of relocating Atlantic Avenue in this central area of the waterfront was to create a traffic-free zone for buildings and people at the water's edge. The relocation was not simple, as it included the removal of a railroad freight line between North and South Station that in the past had served both shipping and the produce market, neither of which remains in this portion of the city.) On our left is one of the new buildings in this central traffic-free area — a hotel (h) on Long Wharf. As we continue easterly along Long Wharf's southern edge, we find the sun on us, we are protected from the wind by the new hotel, and we have a sense of opening to the southeast and the seaward channel. We are delighted by all of the activities this hotel brings to this previously empty waterfront. Furthermore, there are ferries and private boats on the right side of Long Wharf, as well as a new aquarium (i) just across the slip on the next wharf. Continuing easterly along Long Wharf, we pass the old Custom House block (noticing that the recently collapsing T Wharf is no longer there), and shortly thereafter we arrive at the end of Long Wharf (13), with a view of the harbor. Off to our right, to the southeast, we can look again down the seaward channel to the sea itself (14).

If we then look back up the hill along the axis or backbone that we have just traversed, we find several circumferential roads crossing the axis and forming ribs to the axis backbone: Tremont-Cambridge, Congress, and the relocated Atlantic Avenue, all connecting us laterally to the city on either side of the axis, Congress and Atlantic in particular bracing the North End. The axis we have described — along with the roads that cross it and join it to the rest of the city — forms a center of movement that constitutes the combined spatial identity of these two places, Government Center and the waterfront.

In addition to its spatial form, the competence of this place has a temporal component. In the long list of elements that we pass through or touch or see on this axis, there is a remarkable mix of prior times and the present. At one end there is the State House (1798), at the other the timeless harbor and the sea. In between we find the new Government Center Plaza and City Hall (1960s), then Adams Square, Faneuil Hall (1742), the Blackstone block (formed in 1643), Quincy Market (1826; remodeled in the 1960s), State Street, the New Custom House (1837) and its tower (1915), Long Wharf (1710) with its new Hotel Marriott (1975), and the old Custom House block (mid-1700s). This sequence from the State House on Beacon Hill down to the sea ends in a new, granite-paved open space with a view of the harbor and the seaward channel. The older places in this mix have such ties to our beginnings in this city and in

the United States that they add a powerful sense to the area's temporal continuity. To feel this continuity, we have only to look at them alongside of, and in juxtaposition to, those that date from the various periods since the city's founding right up to the present.

As we discussed above, the sixth and seventh ages, of *intimacy* and *generativity,* influenced our work in several ways. The intimate spaces of Boston's old streets were preserved because we understood that intimate spaces give us pleasure. There is generativity of spatial order. In developing the design for these two projects and seeing them as linked, we sought to draw on the imprint of the fabric of the past and, to whatever degree possible, to extend it into the form of what was to be done. Part of that is tied up in how we saw the emerging sense of identity of the place. Part is also in the dominant directionalities of the street: in circumferential ones around Beacon Hill and radial ones connecting Beacon Hill to the harbor and the North End. And part is in the size and shape of the new spaces and how they are linked with the prior ones. First, there is the tying of both the Old Granary Burial Ground space (1 in figure 126) and the space (2 in the figure) that surrounds King's Chapel to the proposed Government Center Plaza space (3 in the figure) by means of the circumferential streets. Second, there is the tying of the proposed Government Center Plaza with the radial direction of the "walk to the sea," which as we have seen runs from the State House to Long Wharf and the harbor. Third, there is the size of the spaces proposed and their relation to the spaces in the existing fabric. We thought the space occupied by the important proposed Government Center Plaza (3) might be twice the size of the Old Granary Burial Ground (1) and the space around King's Chapel (2), without seeming too large. Several other local spaces are roughly the same size as spaces (1) and (2): the space (6) flanking the State House, New Pemberton Square (7), and Samuel Adams Square (8). Also, Harborside Park (11) and the space (12) formed by State Street and Long Wharf are approximately the size of space (3), the proposed Government Center Plaza.

In summary, we sought to give these places for our own lives enough richness, identity, character, and intensity that subsequent generations would understand the incredible importance of them to us and would continue to make them valuable resources in their own lives, habitats, and ongoing generativity. We hoped that members of each subsequent generation would revere the past by making it part of themselves. This does not mean they must copy it, however; with an understanding and reverence for the past, they should now be capable not only of making their own present, but of looking to the future as well.

Chapter 3
Historical Continuities

Although we inherited our approach to forming places and buildings from ancient cultures, the recent agrarian age of some short 9,000 years has been the predominant influence of recent years. At the center of this culture lies the deep and overriding attachment to the life-supporting land — what Joseph Campbell refers to as the "seeded earth."[27] For some 3.8 million years, before the rise of agrarian culture, we were hunters and gatherers with deep attachment to the animals we hunted and that supplied us with food. We were a nomadic society, traveling with herds of wild animals. These wonderful life-sustaining animals were celebrated by paintings on cave walls and ceilings. The hunters and gatherers dressed as animals and had the magical thought that by seeming to be them, they became one with them. This nomadic life of hunting, gathering, and worshipping of animals formed this culture's continuity (figures 127–129).

129 Contemporary Bushman eland dancer, Africa: Aspects of the ancient hunter/gatherer culture persist in modern times.

127 Cave painting in the Cave of the Three Brothers, Montesquieu-Aventes, Pyrenees (see detail at right)

128 Detail of the shamanlike figure

130 *Contemporary agrarian landscape, Aroostook County, Maine*

About 9,000 years ago, people began raising animals and planting grain in order to procure food. These innovations so radically changed the way we used our energy, so greatly increased the size and the constancy of our food source, that we changed our ecological niche — the only creature on the planet ever to have done so. This cultural change meant that we needed to demonstrate our profound commitment to the earth. By existing harmoniously with the seeded earth and by nurturing it, we hoped to invoke the good powers — Mother Nature, the goddess of fertility, the rain gods — and by so doing to ward off the bad powers. We sought to prevent our own destruction and natural disasters of frost and drought, flood and fire. We demonstrated our intent to live in harmony with the earth not only through our daily conduct and the arrangement of our agrarian environment, but also through the sacrifice of one of our dearest possessions: a goat, a lamb, a bull, even a child.

As farmers with all our resources in one farm, we needed to show a harmonious self — our family, house, and farm — before the eyes of the gods. We therefore arranged the pastures and fields, the orchards, fences, walls, shed barns, and houses all in a way that was continuous, and suggestive of a harmonious community of elements. We were attached to the land and celebrated it. We were a part of it and supported by it (figures 130–132).

For much of those 9,000 years, the elements that made up agrarian places and buildings were of necessity made entirely of local materials. In some places masonry dominated; in others, timber; in some, a combination of the two. Whatever materials were put to use (in New England: timber, purlin, board, clapboard, or shingle, for example), there was a dominant agrarian order in the buildings that were constructed. Each element was seen as sincere, a well-found and well-used piece of material. Each had its own worthy role to perform in the construction of the building. And every element had a secondary assignment to aid adjacent elements in the assembly process and to develop firmness. (The post's mortise, for example, would receive the beam's tenon.) Each element was subordinate to the overall purpose and form of the building, which in turn was subordinate to the overall ordering of the farm. All of this was under the direction of the farmer, who both made — or inherited — and used it. The farmer, in turn, sought the approval of the

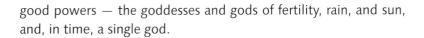

131 Harvesting a family farm

good powers — the goddesses and gods of fertility, rain, and sun, and, in time, a single god.

For a large part of the Western world, it was from this agrarian, hierarchical, god-centered order that we have inherited a root sense of how to build and make places. This sense involves traditions that we follow. At times we may have departed from them or deconstructed them and started new ones, but we usually acted with respect for this agrarian tradition. Because of this inheritance, our buildings were permanent and fixed artifacts while the nomadic hunter and gatherers lived in various caves or tents. Second, our buildings were clearly differentiated inside from outside for reason of shelter or defense. Third, they formed a continuity with the earth. Fourth, a building was organized as a complete and autonomous whole, though it might be expanded or become part of a group of buildings. Fifth, a building was formed about a central axis in the image of the farmer and the god and was made up of parts that had a harmonious coexistence, one among others. Only in the last few hundred years have we departed from the deep sense of order we inherited from our agrarian past.

132 Winter scene of New England farmyard by Chauncey Ryder

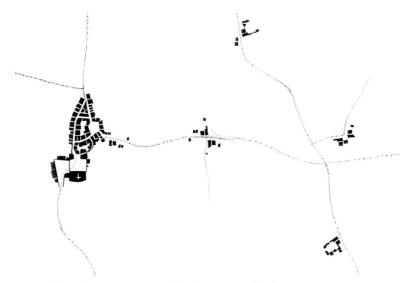

133 Village formation in a medieval, agrarian landscape

134 Map of Old Town, Prague

At some point, clusters of these farm buildings grew into larger communities. In the mid-agrarian period, 4,000 to 5,000 years ago, the clustering of farms began to become villages organized about a common way or street (figure 133). These villages became towns and then cities. Walls were often needed to defend against raids by roving aggressors. Prague, which dates back 1,400 years, is an example of such a city. It was situated on a trade route–river crossing (figures 134–136). A bridge was built across the river and the city's edges were defended by both a bend in the river and the walls and moats built around those edges.

The expense of building walls, moats, and bridges put economic pressure on the city to increase the population density and build as much housing and as many service structures within the walls as possible. One-story buildings became two and three stories, sometimes more. Shops, pubs, eateries, and stables occupied the ground floor and living quarters were above. As the city expanded, public ways became narrower and buildings taller. Thus the building units were small and often higher than they were wide. The city inhabitants were contained not only within a defensive wall, a protective river, and a defended bridge, but also by the narrow, twisting public ways. The tall buildings that sprang up on both sides of these public ways made maximum use of limited space (figures 137 and 138).

In all of this early city building there is a quality of closeness imposed by the narrow ways and by use of common materials. Prague has a thick masonry, with respect to both room size and street width. The thickness of the walls that came about from this

135 Charles Bridge, Prague

136 Bridges over the Vltava, Prague

137 Town clock, Prague

138 Old Town, Prague

139 City gate / entry to Old Town

140 Gallery in Old Town, Prague

masonry, combined with relatively small, deep-set windows, created a sense of defense and security within (figures 139 and 140). Inner courtyards allowed for light and air to enter and provided a secondary access and egress to and from the built mass.

Collections of these thick-walled town buildings along narrow, winding ways evoke a lateral continuity that seems similar to the continuities found among a string of farm structures. But there is no continuity evident between the structures in these cities and the earth below such as we saw in the farm buildings. This is because we are so surrounded in these cities by things above the ground — people, goods, horses, vehicles, buildings — that there is little room in our minds for what is underfoot. Little earth is in evidence given the narrowness of the paved way.

The city has a new continuity, drawn initially from the agrarian one. It speaks of the harmonious quality of coexisting things in a hierarchy, all under the direction of a leader: in the case of the farm, the farmer; in the case of cities, the local lord. In the cities it is a lateral continuity of close-packed elements that are often vertical. Although it is striking that there might be such a transformation of the continuity of the "seeded earth" to a lateral one among the parts of early walled cities, it is useful to remember that the "city" people came from an agrarian culture. As the clusters grew into villages, towns, and walled cities, they were built by people who depended on the region's agriculture. They did not have our present-day ease of transportation and finance, which enables us to fill in readily with crops grown in another region if those in our own area fail. Rather, the agrarian's deep concern for crop failure continued

141 Old Town Square, Prague

even after he moved his habitat inside the city. Therefore, his need to demonstrate to the god(s) his harmonious intent remained, and he now fulfilled it by ordering all things harmoniously in the way he did when he resided outside the walls.

In the history of human life we have experienced very different forms of cultural continuity. The first was the hunter/gatherer culture. The second was the agrarian culture, and the third was the preindustrial urban culture. Recently we have experienced a fourth culture, the industrial one. Fast upon us is a fifth cultural continuity: the electronic age. As we enter a period of increasingly rapid change and global population growth, the mass production of food — agribusiness — will be urgent. Mass industrial production of food is a dramatic change from the prior small-farm output. The "farmer" today is not so likely to pray to a god and tell of his harmonious intent to ensure success. This new method of food production will be similar to the present engineering and business management practices. The old agrarian processes, with their powerful continuities seen in the ordering of the landscape and buildings, whether in the country or town, will no longer drive the ordering of the present landscape and habitat. The beliefs about building, which came about as a result of our agricultural past, will no longer instruct our decision making, and these historic continuities will become the only reminder of what has been.

The rapid cultural change resulting from a decentralized family agriculture to one based in industry and agribusiness, to one based in the electronic age has resulted in the loss of the prior agrarian-based order that governed our buildings and our places. We are now confronted with a postindustrial city that is largely empty of the life-centered and reinforcing sense that informed the earlier orders of city building. Now coexisting elements in our city spaces are disparate and have little to do with one another. Generally absent is a substantial sense of community — that there are significant ways in which we are positively attached to each other — and any real underlying vision or dream that an urban existence might be a positive human one. What will replace what we have lost in this process? Joseph Campbell suggests that any communal dreaming that arises to take the place of that which has disappeared from our modern urban surroundings is unlikely to be catalyzed by present-day religion.[28] It is more likely that communal dreams and visions will be generated by artists, who are the closest thing we have to the shamans of earlier time. If this is true, and we believe it is, we need to turn to the artful self — to poets, writers, painters, musicians, filmmakers, dancers, choreographers, sculptors, architects, artful planners, and businesspeople — to inspirit our dreaming, and

think about urban life and the city. The different talents and visions of all of these artists are needed to dream so multiple and diverse a thing as a city. Artists can put forward only propositions about a shared cultural vision. The citizenry will decide what is significant, what turns it on, what art is. Our citizenry is far more plural than it has been in the past.

In the past century architects have sought a new form of continuity. Think of Mies van der Rohe's Barcelona Pavilion; Frank Lloyd Wright's Falling Water; Le Corbusier's Chapel, Ronchamp, France; or Frank Gehry's Guggenheim Museum in Bilbao, Spain. We need to enlarge briefly on each of these, as they, along with the works of other architects and planners, have contributed significantly to the modern sense of continuity in our habitat. The first and earliest of the four, now informally known as the Barcelona Pavilion, was built as the German Pavilion for the World's Fair in 1928–1929.[29] The pavilion presently sits in an open space, the remains of a fairground. This is surrounded by heavily articulated redbrick buildings that are derived from the strongly enclosed, inturned, defensive buildings of the Victorian era. In the presence of the pavilion, they seem old-fashioned and dull. We are immediately drawn to the pavilion on the right and its small service structure on the left (see figures 142 and 143). These structures are linked by a long upright slab of marble, and each structure has a thin, flat roof. The whole project — two structures, the joining upright marble slab, and the space in front of the slab — sits on a handsome travertine plinth that contains a large reflecting pool at its left end. Occasional chrome-covered columns hold up the roof slabs (see figure 144). The two ends of the plinth are defined by enclosing marble walls that are as high as the soffit of the roof slabs of the two buildings. The whole feels contained.

We gain access to the broad open plinth by means of a rather narrow set of steps that bring us up to face the reflecting pool, which turns us to the right, and then we are again turned to the right by a dark marble slab that is part of the pavilion. Following this slab, we find ourselves in the pavilion's central interior space (see figure 144) facing, through glass, the end court noted above, with its opening to the sky. The space here is beautifully defined. It is both fluid and open and yet well contained by the thin slabs of marble that surround it. Between the upright slabs we can move from considerable openness to increasing enclosure, facing the three-sided space of the end court, filled with another reflecting pool in which we discover a lovely stone sculpture of a woman beautifully positioned (figure 145). The pavilion is handsomely furnished with chairs of chrome and leather also designed by Mies van der Rohe — classics that have come to be known as the Barcelona Chairs.

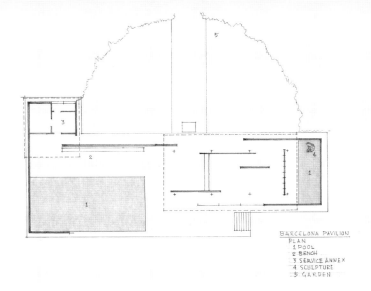

142 Barcelona Pavilion by Mies van der Rohe

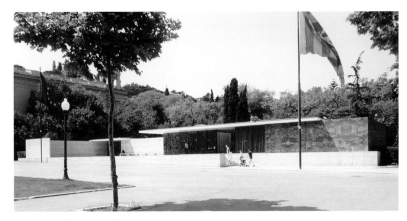

143 Barcelona Pavilion

We become attached to this wonderful space, with its marble slabs and reflecting pool, especially on a clear day with sunlight falling onto the pool and its beautiful sculpture. It is simultaneously fully open and fully contained. It is a magical space. It could not have been achieved in the previous agrarian era.

In time, we find our way out through a narrower space to the rear of the central interior space and reenter the entry court, with its reflecting pool ahead and the defining rear wall to our right; we experience no sharp change as we move from inside to outside. Here we have been introduced to the continuity of modern space. The contrast with the Victorian context could not be more striking. Here is one of the important early sources of the modern spirit of easy, pleasurable openness, visibility, and mobility, an easy connectedness from within to without and vice versa that has energized our lives and habitat and moved us to change from the past. There is little of our architectural past that is like this. The autonomy of spirit with which Mies van der Rohe approached the design of the pavilion and surroundings has given him clarity. He departs from the past by offering us a needed alternative. His initiative has resulted in a space that both is beautiful and connects us centrally to the technology of industry and the emerging mobility of our current culture. Yet despite its novelty, there seems something of the classic Greek in it proportions, its dominant horizontality, its sculptural form, its sculptural centerpiece, its beauty. In creating all of this, Mies van der Rohe has been profoundly generative.

144 Interior, Barcelona Pavilion

145 Sculpture and pool, Barcelona Pavilion

We have already referred to Frank Lloyd Wright's Falling Water, a country house built above and over a small mountain stream in rural western Pennsylvania in 1935 for the Kaufmann family. Its two stories, partly enclosed in glass, partly open balcony, are grounded in a mix of rock ledge and masonry chimney mass and cantilever lightly out over the stream (see again figures 17 and 18). (Beyond the house itself is the vehicular approach — on a bridge just above the house — and a later guesthouse on the wooded slope above the main house.) Although Falling Water has much of the free-flowing space of the Barcelona Pavilion, its continuity is with the natural world of the valley, with the free-flowing space of the forest of hardwoods, with the evergreen ground cover that surrounds it, and with the tumbling stream that flows beneath the house. A stairway hung from the living room above connects us directly to the stream. Europeans seldom mix dwelling with nature, but it is part of the American sense of the modern spatial continuity of our habitat. In 1952, the American Institute of Architects selected Falling Water as "the most important building in America."

Le Corbusier's Chapel at Ronchamp, France, introduces another dimension to our emerging modern continuity. Positioned on top of a hill in a vast, continuous space of open fields, it is a powerful and emotionally moving object in the landscape, with its sloped walls and curvilinear walls and roof, to which we are strongly drawn (figure 146). We have the sense that gravity changes as we approach the chapel. Upon entering, we are taken by the multiple windows piercing the very thick walls, as well as by the powerful

colored glass of those windows (figure 147). There is the sense that this thick-walled, intensely emotional place is here for all times and for all comers. It is modern and sculptural. It draws us to it by its emotional interest and adds another dimension to modernism's involvement with the continuity of free-flowing space, mobility, openness, accessibility, and connectedness between inside and outside. Although there is free-flowing access to the inside, the structure's interior is not visible from without. It is hidden by the walls, suggesting something very valuable within. This is what compels us to enter. As we do, we are given a sacred surprise of shape, light, and color in the powerfully enclosed space in which we find ourselves. The emotional content of the space adds yet another dimension to modernism. In its form, it is beginning to do the work that sculpture, painting, and other visual arts have done in the past. There are in its curved roof and sloped, pierced walls associations with Picasso's *Guernica* mural, the roof form suggesting the horns of the bull and the pierced walls reminding us of the flanks of the bull in bullfighting. Although the structure is clearly modern, it also draws to some important degree from the massive walls and enclosed sacred space of European medieval churches. The chapel evokes an emotional response in a way that painting and sculpture did in the past.

146 *Ronchamp Chapel, by Le Corbusier*

147 *Interior, Ronchamp Chapel*

148 *Riverside façade, Guggenheim Museum, Bilbao, Spain, by Frank Gehry*

Frank Gehry's Guggenheim Museum in Bilbao, Spain, undertakes to contribute to this new modern continuity. Like Le Corbusier's Chapel at Ronchamp, it is a form that evokes a strong emotional response in the viewer (figures 148 and 149). It is a play of fluid forms, of curvilinear volumes and surfaces covered on the outside by shingle-sized pieces of reflective metal (titanium) and on the inside by plaster. These curvilinear forms give a feeling of newness, both inside and out, since our experience has been primarily with rectilinear architectural forms. There is also the emerging association to our own curvilinear bodies. We find ourselves next to, or inside of, what seem to be bigger parts of us, like a shoulder or an abdomen. These curvilinear forms remind us of our fascination with granite ledges, smoothed and curved by mountain streams (see again figures 25 through 28). We can lie on or sit in something curved and smooth like us. Or we can slide down the rocks with the flow of water. Children delight in them, play in them, and love to return there. There is something basic in our connections to such forms. Deep down they are akin to who we are, our own bodies!

149 *Main entrance, Guggenheim Museum*

These four architects were seeking a new continuity. Modernism in architecture and the arts came to Europe, and to a limited degree the United States, after World War I. By the end of World War II, modernism brought an exciting new beginning for the practice of architecture and planning in this country. It projected a world of openness, mobility, light, and space, as well as the suggestion of an energy to do things in a new way: a humanness and creativeness that seemed quite valuable following the darkness of the Depression and the subsequent war. These qualities have been at the center of modernism in general, in its architecture, in its arts, and in its continuity. It is an understanding that lies at the heart of each of the four architectural examples. It is current with and inclusive of our creative energy; our democratic openness in people, buildings, and art; our mobility; the wealth of our industrial center; and our extraordinary technology. These qualities of modernism are only the beginning of a new continuity — a continuity that differs from the agricultural one — and each of the four architects has contributed to this continuity in different ways. Other architects, planners, and artists are presently seeking a new continuity, a new vision for our places that grows from our new and changed world.

There are many profound questions to be addressed by recent, rapid cultural changes, globalization, and the resulting alterations in our places. How can we find attachment in the "lonely crowd"? How can urban/suburban dwellers find continuity and community when they are in constant movement? What will move peoples to get along with each other? How can we Americans provide a safety net for the disadvantaged? How can we see that they are a part of us? How can we preserve the planet from pervasive conflict as the world's population doubles in the next thirty years? How can we change our social milieu from one with an overriding sense of "the lonely crowd" to one of "the crowd with friendly warmth"? How can we move from a culture of fear to one of possibility? Can our artful selves help us with these questions without depending on one good god or one good Father to do it for us?

Although the answers to these questions lie outside the fields of art, architecture, urban design, and psychology, they must come from within our culture. It is vital that these creative fields contribute their share of answers to these questions. For our part, we have two suggestions. First, we recommend the celebration of attachment of one to another, not only the primary attachments between people, but also the great run of lesser ones. We include those between acquaintances, places, buildings, and other artifacts, and by analogy the attachment of building to building and place to place. We envision an urban field of lateral attachment, a lateral continuity connecting us to that which is next to us, and connecting one good thing to another. Celebrating such attachments is of particular import to human survival in an increasingly filled global niche. It serves our need to find a human presence and warmth beyond ourselves, as opposed to an unresolved, inharmonious adversity. As we have shown, harmony that is achieved through the resolution of conflicting tendencies is deeply meaningful to us. Second, we encourage the search for precedent for our habitat — continuity. Although the previous agrarian order of building is different from ours at root, it informs us with some of its successes, in particular its medieval lateral urban continuities that we find so positive and pleasing. As we look to the future, then, we need to value the past so that we can make harmonious and continuous communities that are truly places for people.

Chapter 4
Conclusions

In the foregoing, we have explored the underlying ways in which we are connected to our places. Why are places so important to us and why do we respond positively to some and negatively to others? Places, we have shown, are important in several ways. First, we are never without a place. We may choose to leave a bad or indifferent one or seek a good one, but we are never without one. They are important to our living, as they may be both supportive and reinforcing or just dull or hostile. They may diminish our sense of self and our sense of what we are about, and they may actually hinder our endeavors. In all these ways they make an important difference in our well-being, either for us or against us. They form our earliest experiences. In fact, in the earliest period of our lives they are "us." As infants we are one with place and a part of it, the womb, the mother's arms, the cradle. Only gradually do we to some degree separate from these early "places." Our post-infancy needs of place evolve out of those first experiences of place, additively and progressively, through the diverse "ages" of our lives, creating a set of needs that are as powerful for each of us as are those life experiences in which they were formed. Although these life experiences will be varied and different for each of us, the explorations we have offered suggest that there is a set of needs regarding place that all of us share in varying degrees.

It seems that if a place does not meet one or the other of this set of needs, the part of us that has that need is not recognized in that place, and it is therefore not a good place. For example, if a place is made of materials that do not weather or erode or otherwise show loss or restitution, then it is not such a good place in which to suffer grief, because it offers little to comfort us in loss. The impervious structure of glass, plastic, and steel is one such place. Better, a building with some age to it with its adaptations, settlements, weathering. We are not then alone, but rather with a place that feels a bit like we do. As another example, a place that has an unclear identity is not a place where we want to be — just as a person without an identity is someone we avoid. The expressive content of places can be found in all types of spaces and buildings, from houses, to churches, to government buildings, to public squares, to towns and cities and regional landscapes.

Finding the connection between self and place led us to recognize that habitat making is grounded not only in our inner psychological needs but in historical precedence as well. Modernism did not always create a meaningful continuity. The designs of single buildings did not produce a positive collective form of a street, a neighborhood, a village, or a community.

As we develop our own habitat with a continuity as rich as those of previous eras, we can envision three ways to begin such an undertaking. The first came about in the process of finding images needed to accompany the text. Although we drew from many sources, we increasingly noticed that the images in Edward Steichen's *The Family of Man*[30] were repeatedly to the point (that is, in match with our point). It seems that Steichen, in picking now this image and now that from a collection of photographs drawn from the world over, has a pervasive view that is not compromised by gender, race, wealth, social position, or age. It is a point of view with the persistence of emotion, the emotion that fills them, and how valuable, sincere, profound, wonderful, vulnerable, and mortal all humans are! How sacred they are to us! If there are gods, they are in us! Out of this work by Edward Steichen, with its introduction by Carl Sandburg, there flows a powerful sense of humanity. Out of this sense of humanity may flow an inclusive continuity of our world and culture and in turn a continuity of our place and our habitat.

Second, we should let the agrarian continuity of the past inform us about its successes. As we look to the future, we must value the past and learn from it, so that we can make harmonious and continuous communities that are truly places for people.

The third thought in developing this rich continuity is the subject of this book, which with the help of Erik Erikson attempts to *connect affect with place*. This is what place makers must do. Yes, as designers we want a place that is emotionally rich. Yes, as designers we have some sense for that. As we expand the affective richness of our places, however, it is useful to know something of that inner landscape that we are attempting to serve. The caring inhabitant will understand whether or not that richness of place is for her or him, or just for the designer.

Appendix A
The Eight Ages of Man, from Erikson's *Childhood and Society*

Erikson's eight ages of man offer us a limited set of essential life perceptions.[31] Erikson describes the process of human maturation as a process of human development. Each of the eight ages he identifies brings with its arrival its own conflicts, and each age is dependent upon the age that preceded it. These eight ages are the basic sequential ages through which a person passes as he matures to adulthood and old age. Furthermore, Erikson believes that the "person" we become is the product of our conscious, our unconscious, and society's influences on us. This appendix describes each of Erikson's ages, as they form a basis of our discussion of life's relation to the environment.

The first age of life that Erikson describes is the most fundamental prerequisite for a healthy life: *basic trust*. Trust comes from the sense that we have entered the world from the womb to the safe embrace of the mother. This trust is experienced as *attachment*. Through a sense of attachment, the infant is a part of his mother just as he once was in a literal, physical sense within the womb. As she gives consistent and loving care upon which the infant can depend, he learns to rely on the sameness and *continuity* of that care and in so doing comes to trust his mother and therefore learns to trust himself. Having attachment and continuity is essential to gaining basic trust, the first prerequisite of emotional well-being. This basic trust enables a child to make attachments to other people and the objects he needs in order to mature.

The second stage of life is the age of *autonomy*. At an early age, if a sense of basic trust has been established, the child begins to experience his own autonomous will. He learns that there is a "you" and there is a "me." Children emerge from the world of total dependency into a world in which they seek to be autonomous, to control themselves and their environment. They now have options and newly found power to make decisions: to dress or not to dress, to eat or not to eat, to defecate or not to defecate, to step in a puddle or not to step in a puddle. This ability to feel that we can control and have choices is vital to a healthy development, in which we have self-confidence and a sense of well-being.

The third and fourth ages are those of *initiative* and *industry*. The child, having experienced basic trust, grows from a dependent infant into a person in his own right, an autonomous being who feels he can control his world and make choices. Now the task is for him to give up his childish omnipotence, join society, and become a part of a family. The child is now trusting and confident enough to learn to share, to gain skills and knowledge and competency. The child becomes free to initiate actions, to join others, and to dream of becoming grown up through identification with his parents. The child then learns to gain recognition and satisfaction through producing things and acquiring skills and tools for life.

In the fifth age of the life cycle, *identity*, the youth must connect the roles and skills that he has learned in earlier times with opportunities that are available in the world about him. What he has acquired in earlier stages comes together in this age to enable him to meet the demands of becoming an adult and finding an occupation. There is in this age both a sense of continuity and one of standing alone.

The sixth and seventh ages are those of *intimacy* and *generativity*. As a young adult gains a sense of identity, he seeks to fuse that identity with those of others. He is ready for intimacy, which Erikson describes as "the capacity to commit himself to concrete affiliations and partnerships and to develop the ethical strength to abide by such commitments . . ."[32] Through the capacity for intimacy, the individual can take on a partner with whom he or she can mate and conceive and have babies. Or the individual can take on partners in one form of industry or another and thereby be productive, creative, or generative. Generativity is the creation and nurturance of the next generation. For many, it results from intimacy, when they take on a partner and have a family. For others, generativity is expressed through their work, their production. They become creative and generative without producing offspring. For still others, generativity is both the putting of the next generation in place and the creation of ideas or objects.

Having successfully passed through all of these ages and with the requisite capacities of each age mastered, a person enters the final age, that of *ego integrity,* which Erikson describes as the fruit of the preceding seven ages. "Ego integrity . . . implies an emotional integration which permits participation by followership as well as acceptance of the responsibility of leadership."[33] This "age" is one in which a person faces and accepts his own loss: his death. He can accept this serenely, as he has passed on his values, his creations, and his dreams and ideas to those who follow. He has faced loss but gained restitution in the eyes and hearts of those who follow. "Yet, if we speak of a cycle of life," Erikson says, "we really mean two cycles in one: the cycle of one generation concluding itself in the next, and the cycle of individual life coming to a conclusion."[34]

Our purpose in using Erikson's eight stages of life in this book is to seek a human geography in which we can locate regions of our inner landscape and explore their relation to the outer landscape we inhabit, and, more specifically, to our built or planned world. We seek to understand the ways in which the outer world interests us or bores us, pleases and enhances us, or disgusts, frightens, or stresses us. We have combined some stages for the sake of simplicity and elaborated on others. (*Containment* is one elaboration.) We have not shown what results when the eight ages are not mastered. Essentially what we are finding is that basic trust (achieved through attachment and continuity and containment) and a sense of autonomy, initiative, industry, and the attainment of intimacy and generativity are vital to our well-being. If all goes as it should, we experience ego integration, which enables us to accept ourselves and not fear death. These eight ages, a description of our inner landscape, have a significant influence on our associations with our outer environment.

Appendix B
Notes

1 Charles Brenner, *An Elementary Textbook of Psychoanalysis* (New York: Doubleday Anchor Books, 1955), 54–55.

2 Erik H. Erikson, *Childhood and Society* (New York: W. W. Norton, 1985, 35th anniversary edition).

3 Gail Sheehy, *Passages* (New York: Bantam, 1984).

4 Kent C. Bloomer and Charles W. Moore, *Body, Memory, and Architecture* (New Haven: Yale University Press, 1977).

5 Kevin Lynch and Gary Hack, *Site Planning* (Cambridge: MIT Press, 1984).

6 David Reisman, *The Lonely Crowd* (New York: Doubleday, 1953).

7 Thomas Ansler, Dieter Herrmann, Knut Lohrer, and Ulfert Weber, *Corippo* (Stuttgart: Karl Kramer Verlag, 1959). Translation by Sylvia Davatz.

8 Andrea Palladio, *Four Books on Architecture* (Venice: n.p., 1570).

9 Peter Smith, *Architecture and the Principles of Harmony* (London: RIBA Publications, 1987), 71–73.

10 Bernard Berenson, *The Italian Painters of the Renaissance* (London: Phaidon Press, 1952).

11 Lynch and Hack, *Site Planning,* 72.

12 Erikson, *Childhood and Society,* 261–62.

13 Gaston Bachelard, *The Poetics of Space* (Boston: Beacon, 1958).

14 Bloomer and Moore, *Body, Memory, and Architecture,* 49.

15 Kevin Lynch, *The Image of the City* (Cambridge: MIT Press, 1994), 78.

16 Kevin Lynch, *What Time Is This Place?* (Cambridge: MIT Press, 1972), 1.

17 Erikson, *Childhood and Society,* 263.

18 Josef Albers, quoted in Hermann Zapf, *Manuale Typographicum* (Cambridge: MIT Press, 1968).

19 Herbert Muschamp, "It's Something New under the Stars," *New York Times* (Boston ed.), February 13, 2000, Arts and Leisure, 1.

20 Erikson, *Childhood and Society,* 268.

21 Ibid., 269.

22 Ibid.

23 Rita Rainsford Rouner, "A Short While towards the Sun," lecture for the Boston University Institute for Philosophy and Religion Series *If I Should Die: Life, Death and Immortality,* March 22, 2000, 6.

24 Eric E. Lindermann, "Symptomatology and Management of Acute Grief," *American Journal of Psychiatry* 101 (1944), 141–48.

25 Roger Trancik, *Finding Lost Space* (London: Van Nostrand Reinhold, 1986).

26 Members of Arrowstreet Inc. who worked on the two dormitory projects: John R. Myer, Partner in Charge; Robert Slattery; Linos Dounias; et al.

27 Joseph Campbell, *The Way of the Seeded Earth* (New York: Harper and Row, 1988).

28 Joseph Campbell with Bill Moyers, *The Power of Myth* (New York: Doubleday, 1988).

29 The Barcelona Pavilion was built from 1928 to 1929. It was destroyed in 1930 and rebuilt in 1986.

30 Edward Steichen, *The Family of Man* (New York: Museum of Modern Art, 1955).

31 Erikson, *Childhood and Society,* 247–74.

32 Ibid., 263.

33 Ibid., 269.

34 Erik H. Erikson, *Insight and Responsibility* (New York: W. W. Norton, 1964), 132.

Appendix C
Illustrations

Acknowledgments

We are very grateful to the Ernest A. Grunsfeld Memorial Foundation for its support of the project in its beginning stages.

We are especially indebted to Richard Fahey, social worker, who spent time with us as we began to write, helping us to organize our thoughts. Carla Breeze, photographer; Margaret dePopolo, head of Rotch Library, Massachusetts Institute of Technology; Merrill Smith, Rotch slide librarian; Dr. Robert Reid, psychiatrist; and J. Michael Polan, author and professor at the University of California, Berkeley, all gave us support and concrete help from the beginning.

We want to thank the Graham Foundation for Advanced Studies in the Fine Arts for its generous financial assistance.

Thomas Vietorisz, professor of economics and planning at Cornell and Columbia, was very helpful as the book progressed. Through our lectures to his students, we received useful critiques.

Tom and Athena Hotley gave us advice on book design and publishing, and we are grateful for their continual support and encouragement.

Readers of our late drafts encouraged us and made useful suggestions: Rebecca Sinkler, editor emerita, *New York Times Book Review;* David Sinkler, photographer; Joseph Nye, dean emeritus, Kennedy School, Harvard University; Jan Wampler, professor of architecture, MIT; Shun Kanda, senior lecturer, MIT; and John De Monchaux, dean emeritus, School of Architecture and Planning, MIT.

Our copyeditor, Doris Troy, did a wonderful job improving the text. We are very grateful to Peter and Deidre Randall, who helped us publish and market our book. Sylvia Davatz helped us by translating.

This book would never have taken shape or been so well published without the sensitive help of our book designer, Bruce Kennett. He made many editorial corrections, contributed beautiful photographs, and created a design that added greatly to the book's contents. Working with him was a delight.